DBT Anger Management Workbook

A Complete Dialectical Behavior Therapy Action Plan For Mastering Your Emotions & Finding Your Inner Zen | Practical DBT Skills For Men & Women

By Barrett Huang

https://barretthuang.com/

FREE Guide: Mastering DBT Essentials

FREE DOWNLOAD ALERT!

Master Dialectical Behavior Therapy Skills in 5 Simple Steps with my Free DBT Quick Guide. Access the 'Mastering DBT Essentials' quick guide at:

https://barretthuang.com/dbt-quick-guide/

Or scan the code below:

Table of Contents

Introduction

*"Anger is an acid that can do more harm to the vessel in which
it is stored than to anything on which it is poured."*
– Mark Twain

When I was 16 years old, I had a part-time job at Pizza Hut. I was happy to have that job because I was saving up for extra spending money for college.

At one point, I was working at a different location, covering for someone. I don't exactly remember why, but it was SUPER BUSY one Friday evening. There wasn't enough staff to handle the deluge of orders, so the lines kept growing, and people who had already ordered were becoming more and more impatient because their food was taking too long to arrive.

I had the great luck of being at the front taking orders. This meant I was mostly the recipient of all those impatient glares and occasional rude remarks, so I would call out to the back every now and then to follow up on orders.

I don't know what exactly triggered me. I don't remember a specific remark or anything. But I guess I was flustered because I suddenly whirled around to my colleagues at the back and SCREAMED at the top of my lungs that they should HURRY.THE.H***.UP!!! I then grabbed one of the soft drinks on the tray in front of me, threw it against Jack* , and asked him in a VERY loud voice for everyone to hear if he was stupid or something because he was holding everyone up (not true at all).

---

* Not his real name.

Everyone in the store became quiet. I could feel my face all red and my jaw clenching. I angrily turned back to the next customer in line, and to this day, I remember him looking at me and saying, "*Dude, chill out. It is all good.*" I proceeded as if nothing had happened, and the store slowly returned to normal.

As what often happens, I felt a deep sense of guilt, shame, and remorse after lashing out. After the shift, I looked for Jack* to apologize, but he had already gone home. The following day I was back at the Pizza Hut store where I originally worked, and that was that. (Miraculously, no one reported me.)

No, I didn't look for Jack* to say sorry. I wasn't brave enough for that, but every time I remember that incident, even now, 20 years later, I still cringe in shame.

I would be lying if I said that was the only time I lashed out. Looking back, **I was a very angry teen**.

I was angry at my parents. I am angry about why they bothered to migrate from China to Canada 'to have a better future' when, in my eyes, all they did was live in the past. As a result, I felt that our family never really belonged in Canada.

I was angry at the loneliness I felt every day at school because I didn't have a single friend. I am angry for being different from everyone else.

I was angry at myself because I could feel the anger underneath my skin's surface. My mind recognizes it is not right, and my heart doesn't want me to be angry—but I can't help it.

I was angry at the world. I believed life was unfair, and I didn't see many prospects ahead of me. I was not a teen excited about the future.

I wish I could tell you, dear reader, that a light bulb moment came, and I miraculously stopped being angry. But that's far from the truth.

In reality, I was suffering from a host of mental health issues for most of my adolescent life, and ANGER was one of the ways I manifested my mental health problems.

You see, my father had a hoarding disorder. He kept everything and couldn't let go of anything, so our home was one chaotic mess! He also had Obsessive-Compulsive Disorder (OCD). He always needed things to be a certain way and in a certain spot. He would get very angry and aggressive if things weren't in the right order.

On the other hand, my mother had General Anxiety Disorder (GAD). She was always worrying about... well, pretty much everything. She was always afraid something bad would happen. And since life is not all sunshine and rainbows, when something negative did happen, my mother would be the first one to blame everyone else. She was always playing the victim.

This was my home situation. This was my normal.

As I went to school and saw other kids, I noticed how different things were for other people. I started to compare, resulting in A LOT of conflict and unrest inside me. Since my parents were emotionally absent and I had no friends, there was no one to ask for help. (Truth be told, I wouldn't even know where to begin to describe things!)

Ultimately, it is no surprise that I grew up as an adult with OCD and GAD. I also suffered from depression. But underneath it all, ANGER was always present.

Mostly, my anger was just underneath the surface. Other times though, it would erupt like a volcano, and I would get aggressive towards others. This, of course, would be followed by extreme remorse, which fueled my anxiety and depression even more! I was caught in a loop of anger and misery.

I didn't begin to heal until I left home for college.

At this time, I knew deep down that something was not quite right and realized I needed help. I started seeing professionals in the mental health field, and I was prescribed anti-anxiety medication, which helped me cope a bit with everyday life. But this was just the beginning of my journey.

Again, I wish I could tell you I was on the right path to mental healing from the get-go, but I wasn't. It is true what they say: healing is not a linear process; there are many ups and downs. But this I know to be true: **every step is progress**.

I tried various types of therapy. But the one that worked for me, allowing me to cope and overcome my various mental health and anger issues, is the one I am sharing with you in this book—Dialectical Behavior Therapy (DBT).

DBT really unlocked something inside me. It is very different from the other types of therapy I tried, and I credit it for teaching me the techniques and skills I so desperately needed in life. Today, my anxiety, OCD, depression, and anger problems no longer take over my life.

My journey has inspired me to learn more about the mind and behavior. So I majored in psychology and have completed the DBT Skills certificate program of Dr. Marsha Linehan, the founder of DBT. I have also deepened my knowledge of philosophy, happiness, and self-improvement. Still, I'd like to emphasize that the contents of this book draw primarily from my personal struggles with anger and how DBT helped me cope and manage it. I sincerely hope that it helps you as you take your journey to healing.

Who Should Read This Book

This book is for anyone who's struggling with anger issues in their lives. Please note that anger in itself has a purpose. So the goal is not to completely get rid of it. However, there's a line between healthy anger and problematic anger, anger and rage, anger and out-of-control fury, anger and aggression, and so on.

Unhealthy anger is very draining, and as mentioned in the quote above, it does more damage to you (the vessel of anger) than your intended targets. In short, your anger hurts YOU more than anyone else. This book is for those who don't want to suffer the weight and burden of their anger anymore.

Goals of This Book

This book aims to teach you DBT skills for dealing with and managing anger so that it does not control your life. However, it is also critical to identify the source of your anger. Why are you angry? What (or who) are your triggers? What exactly does your rage mean? Once you understand your anger inside out, you'll find it easier to apply the DBT skills you'll learn in this book to manage your anger.

How to Use This Book

The first part of this book discusses dialectical behavior therapy (e.g., its history, what it entails, what skills are involved, etc.) so that you understand what makes this particular therapy different from other types of therapy. It is important to remember that learning is more than just knowing something. Real learning happens when you apply, use, and engage with your knowledge. As such, DBT worksheets will be provided at the start and throughout this book so that you fully adopt DBT skills in your life.

The second part of this book is all about anger. Anger is not just an emotion or feeling but a *reaction*. It is an emotional, mental, and physical reaction. To what? You'll find out as you go through the pages of this book. This part will truly be a journey within yourself.

The final part of this book is where it all comes together. It is how to use DBT skills to cope, manage, and eventually let go of out-of-control or destructive anger in your life.

Anxiety, loneliness, and anger dominated my childhood and adolescent years. As I grew older, my anger took center stage more and more. I never wanted to accept it, but it is true: it is easier to be mad than to be sad.

Fortunately, I sought help and was lucky enough to eventually find the therapy that worked for me. Today, whenever I look back, I no longer feel rage. I only feel empathy for my younger self.

So let this be my message to you before you read further:

PLEASE BE KIND TO YOURSELF

You deserve kindness, understanding, and compassion, just like everyone else. You are not your anger. Your anger is a reaction to something. And during this journey, you will figure it all out. But don't rush anything, put too much pressure on yourself, or go on this path for the sake of others. Just be kind to yourself and focus your time and energy on making yourself feel better. The rest will follow.

What is Dialectical Behavior Therapy?

"You have the power to heal your life, and you need to know that. We think so often that we are helpless, but we're not. We always have the power of our minds... claim and consciously use your power." – Louise L. Hay

Dialectical Behavior Therapy, or DBT, was developed by Dr. Marsha Linehan[1], Ph.D., in the 1980s as a result of her and her colleagues' work with patients with borderline personality disorder (BPD).

Working with BPD patients who were suicidal, Linehan realized that, unlike cognitive behavior therapy (CBT), which focuses primarily on detecting negative thought patterns and changing them to positive ones (*change-focused*), it is far more effective to employ two opposing (*dialectical*) strategies: Acceptance AND Change.

But perhaps what also makes DBT so effective is that Dr. Marsha Linehan suffered from mental health issues herself.[2]

In the 1960s, she was sent to a clinic for "extreme social withdrawal" at just 17 years of age. According to Dr. Linehan, she engaged in various self-harming activities while in the

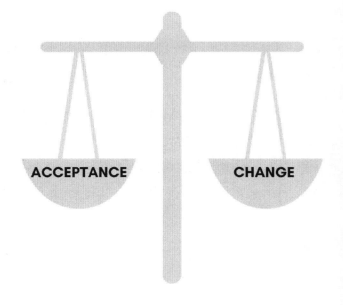

clinic, such as cutting and burning her skin using cigarettes. As such, she was kept in isolation for her own safety.

In the 1960s, borderline personality disorder (BPD) was not yet known, so she was misdiagnosed with schizophrenia and aggressively medicated for it (which, of course, did not help because that was not the mental health issue from which she suffered).

Dr. Linehan was eventually released from the clinic after 26 months, but she was far from better. However, about four years later, she had a sudden insight while praying.

She suddenly realized that she had been attempting to end her life multiple times because the gap between the person she wanted to be and the person she actually was was so huge that it filled her with hopelessness and desperation. She so badly wanted to live a better life, but she didn't know how to bridge that gap... until she realized that Change itself is not enough.

She should also ACCEPT her reality AS IS. No judgments. Her behavior, though destructive, made sense because she was suffering from the weight of her reality at the time. Dr. Linehan would later call this epiphany **Radical Acceptance**.

This part of DBT—Radical Acceptance—is so different from other types of therapy because all it entails is for you to acknowledge your present reality. There's no need to understand it, evaluate it, judge it, twist it, overthink it, or fight it.

RADICAL ACCEPTANCE = IT IS WHAT IT IS

When I first learned about Radical Acceptance, I was taken completely aback. So many of the other therapies I tried focused on answering, *"why are you like this?"* as the first step to healing.

Please don't get me wrong. It is important to understand yourself. But by focusing on *"why are you like this?"* first, it sort of implied that what I was doing was just *"wrong"*. Now, many professionals will argue with this, but as someone who experienced mental health issues, I am saying that this is MY experience. This is how I felt during this phase of therapy. (And please, DO NOT let anyone invalidate your experiences! I had to learn that the hard way.)

I also noticed that the more time I spent attempting to answer the question, *"why am I like this?"* the more time I spent in that frame of mind. So, even though I knew it was a step toward recovery, I didn't feel any better while exploring it. (In all honesty, I felt worse at times since revisiting specific events in my life to better understand them merely made me relive all the feelings involved with them, which made me either angrier or even more miserable because I was full of regret.)

In contrast, with Radical Acceptance, I felt free. This is my reality now. Full stop. Now what?

Well, this brings us to the second foundation of DBT—**Change**.

People don't realize that most of us with mental health problems and anger issues know deep down that we should not think, say, or act the way we do. We can't help but react that way, but a little voice in our heads says, *"Well, that could be better."* But, how?! Isn't that the real question? So many people say, *"Change for the better"*. My struggle was always the HOW of things. Fortunately, DBT showed me how.

In addition to accepting her reality, Dr. Linehan realized that real change is possible by learning new behaviors.

CHANGE = LEARN NEW BEHAVIORS TO LIVE BETTER

Dr. Linehan believed that by changing how we act (or react) to situations, we can change how we feel about them in time. When I first learned this, it made perfect sense to me.

For the most part, we are the by-product of our genes (*nature*) and our environment (*nurture*). There's massive debate over which is more predominant, but I have always been a proponent of nature AND nurture. We are influenced by both. But the *nurture* part that's *conditioning,* and research shows that we can condition ourselves to do anything.[3]

So, DBT's CHANGE principles are the HOWs that you need to cope with and manage your anger issues.

DBT Fundamentals

Dialectic means seeing things from multiple perspectives. In Dialectical Behavior Therapy, Dr. Linehan defines it as "a synthesis or integration of opposites".[4] In particular, it is the synthesis of Acceptance and Change.

Acceptance and Change

Note that there are no first and second steps here. Acceptance and Change (or desire to change) can happen simultaneously. At first glance, this may seem impossible, but is it? A person can be gentle and firm at the same time; someone can exhibit the characteristics of a team player and a team leader at the same time; a person can be angry and still show compassion at the same time.

So, this is the goal of DBT: Accepting your emotions about a situation at any given moment while simultaneously Changing the behaviors that cause you further suffering.

Here's how I put this into practice: I moved away to go to college, but that doesn't mean I never went home for the holidays. My father was still a hoarder suffering from OCD, and my mother was still a woman with anxiety who treated me like a child. For many years, this caused my depression and anger problems to worsen, so I went home less and less.

However, after learning about DBT, my mindset changed. Whenever I went back home, and something unpleasant happened, Radical Acceptance would kick in. I'd just take a moment to acknowledge my anger. Change would then follow in the sense that I would NOT react the same way as I used to because now I know that if I stay in that anger or do something that feeds that anger, I am just prolonging my own suffering.

Before DBT (teen years): Mom enters my room without knocking, re-arranges the papers on my desk, and throws stuff she thinks is useless (oh yes, THAT happened). Since there IS logic to the madness on my desk, even if she doesn't see it, I would get very angry, say hurtful words, and sometimes in a fit of rage, I would be like that *Tasmanian Devil* cartoon character and deliberately wreck my room. Since my mom loves to play the victim, a litany of all their sacrifices would come out. This, in turn, would make me angrier or fill me with remorse (sometimes both). The whole event would, of course, hang like a dark cloud over the family over the holidays, and sometimes, I'd carry it for days on end back at my college dorm. (See? I was prolonging my suffering.)

After DBT (adult years): Mom went to visit my apartment while I was out. It is normal for Asian parents to have keys to their children's homes. What was not normal was when my mom went through my kitchen cupboards and threw out what she considered unhealthy food. When I came back home and saw my cupboards cleared out of all my favorite food, I excused myself. I went to the bathroom to splash cold water all over my face and neck (a DBT technique I'll explain later), and as I looked at myself in the mirror, I made a mental note to install a lockable pantry door where I could stash all my stuff. The End.

Oh, I am not saying it was easy or that things improved overnight. However, by implementing the new behaviors I learned from DBT, many aspects of my life improved, not just my relationship with my parents but also my relationships with colleagues, friends, partners, and, most importantly, myself.

One of the things I truly appreciate about DBT is that it is not all just theory. It offers many exercises so that we can truly understand and adopt its principles. The following are the first of many DBT worksheets throughout this book. I encourage you to accomplish them not just once but over and over until the DBT way of thinking becomes second nature to you.

Worksheet: Acceptance and Change

Everything starts with Acceptance AND Change. The following is an example of how you can start applying these DBT fundamentals in your life.

SELF-ACCEPTANCE: Accept today's reality AS IS.

DESIRE TO CHANGE: Set yourself up to welcome change.

DECLARATION: Acknowledge today and what you want for tomorrow.

SELF-ACCEPTANCE

I AM ANGRY right now.

I AM DOING MY BEST. THAT'S ENOUGH.

Things are not going as planned. That's okay.

It's okay to feel this way.

My anger makes sense to me right now. avalid.

DECLARATION:

"I accept myself as who I am right now. I'm like this for a reason even though I don't know why. What I do know is that I don't feel happy or fulfilled living this way. This is not my best life. So I'm opening myself to learning new things to increase my happiness."

DESIRE TO CHANGE:

I am not as happy as I know I could be.

I AM OPEN TO CHANGE.

My ANGER is not who I am. I want to explore who I am.

I will not feel guilty for wanting to be better.

There's nothing wrong with wanting 'more'.

Now, it is your turn!

SELF-ACCEPTANCE: Write statements acknowledging your circumstances at the moment.

DESIRE TO CHANGE: Write statements that affirm your openness and willingness to change for the better.

DECLARATION: State your acceptance of today AND your desire for a better life tomorrow.

SELF-ACCEPTANCE: **DESIRE TO CHANGE:**

DECLARATION:

DBT Core Skills

DBT is composed of four primary skills: *Mindfulness, Distress Tolerance, Emotion Regulation,* and *Interpersonal Effectiveness.*

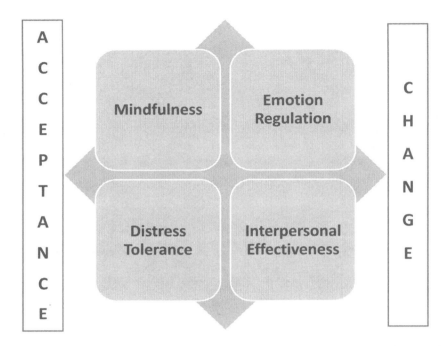

As the above image implies, Acceptance is made possible by adopting *Mindfulness* and *Distress Tolerance* skills, while Change happens by learning *Emotion Regulation* and *Interpersonal Skills.*

Mindfulness

Say Mindfulness, and most people would immediately have a vision of someone meditating on a mat with their eyes closed and their legs crossed. But there's a difference between the two: mindfulness is a state of mind, while meditation is a practice.

Mindfulness is a state of awareness. You are 'awake' and fully present in the moment (not distracted), whatever the situation, whatever you're doing. Meditation is a practice that helps you become more mindful.

In DBT, Mindfulness is split into two aspects – WHAT and HOW.

WHAT Skills

These skills deal with <u>what you need to do to be more mindful</u>.

1. **Observe**: Pay attention to what is going on inside and outside you. Take note of what you're feeling.
2. **Describe**: Explain what you see (observe) in your own words.
3. **Participate**: Be in the moment to get the most out of the experience. You probably don't even notice it anymore, but you're doing A LOT of things simultaneously. For example, you're barely awake, but you're already (1) reaching for your phone while (2) thinking about your work deadlines and (3) your first meeting of the day, while (4) worrying if the kids did their assignments. When was the last time you just focused on waking up?!

HOW Skills

These skills focus on <u>how you can be more mindful every day</u>.

4. **Non-Judgmentally**: When we are mindful of something, we don't need to label or judge it. We simply observe.
5. **One-Mindfully**: Pay attention to one thing at a time. Don't multitask when it comes to awareness.
6. **Effectively**: Evaluate what works best for you today. Things that worked for you in the past may no longer be effective for you. Learn to let go of these "old systems" and do what works for you now.

Mindfulness WHAT and HOW skills aim to educate us on how to notice and experience reality AS IS, to be less judgmental, and to effectively live in the moment.

Worksheet: Mindful Breathing

1) Pick a place where you won't be disturbed.

2) Sit down or lie on a mat or on your bed, whatever is comfortable for you.

3) Close your eyes.

4) Breathe in deeply for a count of four (4), and then exhale for a count of four (4). Do this four (4) more times. (Five rounds in total).

5) On your next inhale, Observe your breath and Describe it.

   • Are you breathing in easily?

   • Do you smell anything? If so, describe the smell. (Important: Describe the smell Non-Judgmentally. Don't give any opinion or say you like the smell or dislike it. Simply describe the smell (e.g., *fresh*, *floral*, *citrusy*, etc.)

6) As you exhale, Observe your hands and Describe them.

   • Where are your hands?

   • Are your hands closed? Semi-curled? Palms up? (Important: Remember to observe and describe One-Mindfully. Don't focus on any other part of your body. Focus solely on your hands.

You can stop here or continue this exercise.

For every inhale and exhale, pick something to Observe and Describe, and remember to do so Non-Judgmentally and One-Mindfully. If you ever find your mind wandering, that's okay. Just re-group, re-focus, and get back on track.

Wise Mind

In DBT, Mindfulness is the skill you need to arrive at Wise Mind, which is the middle ground between our emotional and rational minds.

It is said that we make most of our decisions based on emotions.[5] But acting, reacting, or behaving based on feelings alone, especially negative ones, doesn't always bring out the best in us, nor does it lead to the best situations.

The good thing is that Wise Mind is not something we need to create. We all already have it. Think of it as a muscle that we just need to use more often. With constant effort to use it, relying on Wise Mind will become natural to us.

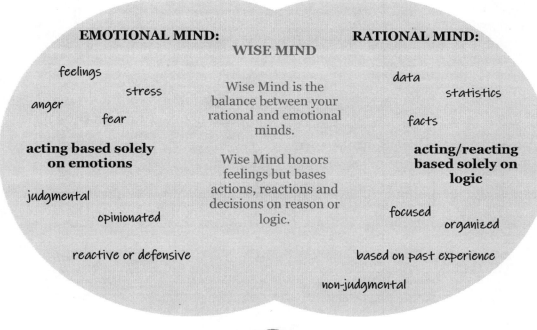

EMOTIONAL MIND:

WISE MIND

RATIONAL MIND:

feelings

stress

anger

fear

acting based solely on emotions

judgmental

opinionated

reactive or defensive

Wise Mind is the balance between your rational and emotional minds.

Wise Mind honors feelings but bases actions, reactions and decisions on reason or logic.

data

statistics

facts

acting/reacting based solely on logic

focused

organized

based on past experience

non-judgmental

Worksheet: Wise Mind

The goal of **Wise Mind** is to help us make sense of our thoughts and feelings so that we can come up with a balanced (Wise) response to events.

EMOTIONAL MIND:

RATIONAL MIND:

WISE MIND

Do what is right while soothing your emotions.

What you <u>want</u> to do

What you <u>should</u> do

1. Think of an event when you regretted your action/reaction/behavior. Be as detailed as possible about the event.

   Example: I shouted at a colleague and stormed out of a meeting because of an argument over our project.

   Your turn:

   _____

   _____

   _____

2. Why did you react that way?

   Example: I was frustrated over the lack of progress in the project.

   Your turn:

   _____

   _____

   _____

3. Why do you regret your action/reaction/behavior?

   Example: It didn't help the situation at all, and my co-workers started avoiding me.

   Your turn:

   _____

   _____

   _____

4. What would you do differently?

   Example: Instead of blaming my colleague and getting angry, I would help come up with solutions. That way, the people would be more motivated about the project.

   Your turn:

   _____

   _____

   _____

Notes: Question #1 above points to a time when you were in Emotion Mind. With the benefit of hindsight, Question #4 points to Wise Mind. Think of other situations when you acted based on Emotion Mind and what you would do differently. With constant reflection, you're practicing how to use Wise Mind.

Distress Tolerance

Distress Tolerance is our ability to face and effectively handle stressful, upsetting, and difficult situations.

When faced with difficult situations, some people tend to ignore, deny or escape what's happening. This may work temporarily, but in the long run, it causes you more harm and does not equip you with the tools you need to handle future crises. Other people, me included, tend to lash out and do something without thinking of its consequences. Our goal is to feel better immediately, not realizing that we've just made the situation worse.

For example, my OCD and anxiety disorders got so bad that, at one point, I avoided stepping on cracks on the pavement. My every step needed to land perfectly. Otherwise, my day was doomed. And if God forbid, I did step on a line or crack on the floor, I would get very frustrated and angry. I would lash out. It didn't matter where I was or who was in front of me. I'd say something mean or throw a fit, and that was that.

Distress tolerance skills helped me tremendously because they taught me how to endure and handle very upsetting situations without making them worse and to accept reality (life as it is *in the moment*, not forever) even though I can't change it and it is not what I want it to be.

The following exercises (Grounding on page 29 and TIPP on page 31) are some of the first DBT distress tolerance skills I learned. I still use them today whenever I feel very upset about something. I hope they help you too.

Worksheet: Grounding Technique Using Your 5 Senses

Grounding techniques connect you to the present so you can disconnect from your worries. Using your five senses—sight, smell, sound, touch, and taste—is an excellent way to ground yourself. Do this exercise anytime you feel stressed, worried, or anxious.

Remember, there is no right or wrong answer here. Don't evaluate or judge anything. Just provide what's being asked.

List FIVE (5) things you can see right now.

Example: desk lamp, water bottle, computer speakers, board marker, keys

1.

2.

3.

4.

5.

List FOUR (4) things you can touch right now.

Example: plate, spoon, fork, apple

1.

2.

3.

4.

List THREE (3) things you can hear right now.

Example: bird, Spotify music, neighbor

1.

2.

3.

List TWO (2) things you can smell right now.

Example: cologne, coffee

1.

2.

List ONE (1) thing you can taste right now.

Example: gum

1.

If you're still feeling in distress, do the exercise again or list down AS MANY things as you can per sense.

Worksheet: TIPP

The following Distress Tolerance exercise focuses on altering your body's chemistry in order to counteract unfavorable or undesirable cravings or emotions. You'll discover that altering your physiological state will enable you to alter your emotional state more quickly.

 Temperature: Anger makes your temperature rise. Counter this by cooling yourself. You can splash your face with cold water, go out in the cold, or you can put your head inside the refrigerator for a few seconds.

 Intense Exercise: Release your anger by exercising intensively. If you don't have much time, apps like the _5 Minute Home Workouts_ by Olson Applications can be used to get in some fast exercise throughout the day. The trick is to press on until your powerful emotions start to subside.

 Paced Breathing: Notice how you tend to breathe rapidly when you're angry? Slow down your anger by taking slow, deep breaths in and out. For example, take 4 seconds to breathe in and 5 seconds to breathe out. **Tip**: Feel free to use apps such as Prana Breath or Breathe to help with this step.

 Paired Muscle Relaxation: Do this while performing Paced Breathing above. When you inhale deeply, slowly contract your muscles (without tensing them to the point where they cramp), then when you exhale deeply, let all that tension go and tell yourself to relax.

Emotion Regulation

Let me start by saying that your feelings are always valid. I truly never liked it whenever someone told me to just '*get a grip*' or '*change your feelings*', or when I am trying to explain something (which is something very hard for me to do) and then have someone casually comment, '*that's not true*'. In my mind, these are MY experiences, MY emotions, MY truths, and so when someone tries to invalidate them, I get very angry.

However, I have come to realize that my emotions are not who I am. My emotions don't have to control me. I am the one who has the power to control (regulate) my emotions.

Now, I know that you should never change for others. That never works. So for a while, I even *resisted* doing something about my volatile emotions and resulting behavior. I thought, "*Well, if I change, that means THEY are right, and I am wrong.*"

But DBT taught me something that changed my way of thinking: if I entertain misery, I stay miserable. If I don't do anything to be happy, I stay unhappy. In short, if I don't do anything to get out of my funk, I am just making myself suffer longer. And I didn't want to suffer any longer. I was tired of my OCD, anxiety, and anger issues. They were dominating and derailing my life, and I truly wanted to live a better life.

So, Emotion Regulation, in many ways, is about understanding yourself. It is about understanding your emotions, why you're even feeling that way, and how to change unwanted emotions and manage extreme emotions—because you no longer want to suffer from them.

IMPORTANT: Emotion Regulation skills are NOT about getting rid of emotions. Emotions are part of what makes us human. So the goal is not to get rid of or invalidate them. The objective is simply to identify emotions that are negative, harmful, or non-beneficial to us and to regulate these feelings so that we feel better about ourselves and life in general.

I won't lie to you. Unlike altering your body chemistry (physical condition), changing your emotional state is more difficult. But I promise you that it can be done! How? Start with the Emotion Regulation exercises below. And please do not do them just once. It takes multiple efforts over time to learn new behaviors, so please keep at it until they become almost second nature to you.

Worksheet: Check the Facts

Check the Facts is an exercise where you pause, reflect, and fact-check your emotions. This helps you make logical sense of a situation (arrive at Wise Mind, page 25) and not overreact.

First, let's do a reflective exercise. Look back and think of a few situations where you overreacted. It can also be an event that, at the time, you thought was a big deal, but it turned out to be unimportant.

Question: What emotion do you want to fact-check?

Example: my anger

Your answer:

Question: What happened? What triggered this emotion?

Example: My sister skipped my bridal shower. I was furious because she was in charge of the party giveaways.

Your answer:

Question: What assumptions did you make about the event?

Example: My sister deliberately tried to ruin my bridal shower.

Your answer:

Question: What did you do?

Example: I sent very angry, accusatory text messages to my sister and told her she was no longer welcome at my wedding.

Your answer:

CHECK THE FACTS!

You listed your assumptions above, but <u>WHAT ELSE</u> happened?

Example: My brother-in-law had an accident at work, and my sister had to rush to his side. She was so distraught she completely forgot about my bridal shower.

Your answer:

Question: Why do you think you reacted that way? What were you afraid of?

Example: My sister and I have not been on the best of terms for years, and although things were a lot better, I was afraid it was just all a façade, and she was still out to get me.

Your answer:

Question: Looking back, on a scale of 0-5, did your emotion fit the facts? (0 = not at all, 5 = yes):

Example: 0, not at all

Your answer:

Question: If your emotion DID NOT fit the facts, what would you do differently?

Example: I would not jump to conclusions and give her the benefit of the doubt. I would also not have acted on my emotions and sent those angry text messages.

Your answer:

Question: If your emotion DID fit the facts, would you do anything differently?

Example: Yes. I would not have acted impulsively and sent angry text messages to my sister because by letting my anger get control of me, I ruined my bridal shower for myself. Instead of enjoying the party and my friends, I was consumed by anger at my sister throughout the event.

Your answer:

IMPORTANT: Check the Facts can be used whenever you're in a negative situation. It is not just for past events. However, I suggest you do the above exercise at least two (2) more times. That is, think of past events when you may have overreacted and, as a result, made the situation worse. This is to get you accustomed to the process of fact-checking your emotions.

Worksheet: Opposite to Emotion

Sometimes, even when we fact-check our feelings and find that our emotions do not match the facts, we still want to do what we want to do instead of what we should do.

To prepare you for such situations, below is an **Opposite to Emotion** table. Column A lists down unhealthy emotions; on Column B, write down what you would normally want to do when you feel these emotions; and then, on Column C, write an *opposing action* to your original natural urge.

The next time an unpleasant situation occurs, refer to this table and do what you wrote in Column C. (I have done the first emotion as an example for you.)

A	B	C
Emotion	**Emotion-Driven Behavior**	**Opposite Action**
What you are feeling.	*What you would normally do because of this emotion. (If your natural urge is to do something other than what's listed below, please list them on a separate sheet.)*	*Write down an opposite action to what you're feeling.*
Sadness	*Self-isolate; not want to be with anyone at all*	*Call a few friends and meet up with them.*
Guilt	Shut down, self-criticize, or even blame others (deflect)	
Anger	Shout, sulk, do something aggressive like breaking something	
Fear	Run away from a situation	

A	B	C
Emotion	**Emotion-Driven Behavior**	**Opposite Action**
What you are feeling.	*What you would normally do because of this emotion. (If your natural urge is to do something other than what's listed below, please list them on a separate sheet.)*	*Write down an opposite action to what you're feeling.*
Emptiness	Binge-eat	
Loneliness	Get back together with a toxic ex, say sorry to a friend even though it is not my fault just so we can be friends again	
Frustration	Throw things around the room	
Helplessness	Cry and feeling depressed	
Resentment	Talk ill about someone/something	
Feel free to add more emotions and scenarios in the extra rows below.		

Interpersonal Effectiveness

Relationships are important in life. They provide the foundation for our overall happiness and well-being.[6] A meta-analysis of 148 studies revealed that people with strong social interactions have a 50% lower risk of early death.[7] Healthy connections also allow us to recover more quickly after stressful experiences because we know we have the support of others.

DBT's Interpersonal Effectiveness skills focus on creating and sustaining healthy relationships not just with others but with ourselves. You see, often, in our desire to be in good standing with others, we tend to give in too much and lose ourselves. This is not healthy for us in the long run.

So, Interpersonal Effectiveness is actually all about balance. We learn to prioritize ourselves and respect our own wishes (**ME**) while at the same time considering the needs and desires of others (**THEM**).

When we know how to balance ME + THEM, then we can strengthen our current relationships, learn how to find and keep new relationships, and are able to end unhealthy or toxic relationships.

One of the most powerful things I have learned under this DBT skill is that often, I don't get what I want out of a situation because I do not know how to ask for them effectively. I either demanded something, which of course, rubbed the other person the wrong way making them unwilling to give in to my request, or I was not assertive enough and let people walk over me. In both situations, I don't get what I want, which, of course, would anger me.

Hopefully, the following DBT exercises will help you as much as they helped me in my relationships.

Worksheet: FINDING FRIENDS

As much as we'd like to believe otherwise, relationships don't just happen. Often, we have to work to find people we like and exert effort to get them to like us. Accomplish the following worksheet to help you find friends and keep them to reduce any feelings of isolation or loneliness.

 # 1. Find close opportunities. It is easier to find friends and keep them if you know you'll have regular contact with them. So list down at least three (3) places that you frequent where you can meet new people.

Examples: at school, at the office, at the local Starbucks

Your turn:

1. _____

2. _____

3. _____

 # 2. Find similarities. It is easier to make friends with people who already like some of the same things that we do. And it is easier for the other person to like us in turn because research shows that we all tend to like people who remind us of ourselves.[8,9,10] When you do find them, let that be your conversation starter!

Example: "Hi, I couldn't help but overhear you're into cooking reality shows? Cool! Me too. Do you watch MasterChef?"

Your turn:

_____

_____

_____

 # 3. Practice good conversation skills. If you're an introvert like me, it is hard to not only start a conversation with someone but also to keep it going! Following are some important tips to keep in mind.

- **Ask and respond.** Practice the art of ending your conversations with a question. Keep in mind, though, that since you just met the person, ask general questions. For example, *"This is not the first time I have seen you here. **Do you live nearby**?"* is too personal, and the other person will most likely not be comfortable sharing something so private yet. So keep the conversation light.

  Example: I noticed you ordered the Caramel Macchiato. This is my first time visiting this café, any other recommendations?

  Your turn:

  _____

  _____

  _____

- **Engage in small talk.** It may sound silly but small talk is exactly what's required when meeting someone new.

  Examples:
  - *Amazing day, isn't it?*
  - *Don't know about you, but it is those sinful cronuts that make me come here all the time. How about you?*
  - *You work at [company]? Do you know Mike over there at Accounting?*

  Your turn:

  _____

  _____

  _____

- **Share 'just enough'.** Just as you don't want to ask personal questions, it is equally important not to overshare too. Simply put, you guys are not at that stage yet, so it is best to share 'just enough' about yourself. If you're not sure, take your cue from the other person.

Examples:

YOU: I don't know about you, but it is those sinful cronuts that make me come here all the time. How about you?

NEW FRIEND: Oh, they look way too sinful for me. But I can't help myself from ordering the French Toast every morning!

YOU: Ah, a breakfast person, me too! But I am not into anything sweet in the morning. What would you recommend instead?

Your turn:

_____

_____

_____

- **Don't interrupt.** No one likes to be interrupted. Even though you're just excited to agree with the other person, don't jump into the conversation too quick because it gives the impression that you're not listening to them. Think of a few ways you can train yourself to stop interrupting people. (I have filled in the first few lines to give you an example.)

  1. *Pause for 5 seconds before speaking.*
  2. *Repeat what they said when they're done speaking before you say what you want to say. (Example: Wow, did you just say you like French Toast too?)*
  3. *Bite your inner lip to prevent yourself from interrupting.*
  4. _____
  5. _____
  6. _____
  7. _____
  8. _____
  9. _____
  10. _____

- **Prepare some discussion points.** *What to talk about?* This is often what stomps people from meeting someone and carrying on a conversation. Personally, because of my anxiety disorder, I would really overthink this. It is like I can't relax and just be in or enjoy the conversation because some part of my brain is already trying to plan the next topic. To get over this, I had to go 'back to basics'.

  Let's go back to the first item in this worksheet, i.e., **Find close opportunities.**. So this actually narrows down the *where*, right? From here, just come up with a few general topics that fit the situation.

  For example, if you plan to meet new people at your **corner coffee house**, then the discussion points could be about the *local neighborhood, coffee specialties, baristas, the coffee shop menu,* etc. If you want to introduce yourself to a **co-worker**, then discussion points could be about a *work project, a looming deadline, a new colleague or boss, how you (or they) ended up working there,* etc.

I know it is hard to find friends, but be brave! If we wait for people to come to us, we may never have friends. So, have the courage to put yourself out there. Remember, no risk, no reward.

Worksheet: DEARMAN

DEARMAN helps you get your messages across without damaging your relationships. It helps you be more assertive while keeping the other person's feelings in mind. Fill out your response against each acronym in the spaces provided below.

 escribe the situation.

When you are describing an incident or situation, do so clearly. Avoid mentioning your opinions and stick to the facts.

Example: I have been working beyond my hours, without overtime pay, for the third week now.

Your turn:

_____

_____

 xpress how you are feeling about the situation.

Use **'I'** statements when communicating. **'You'** statements can be taken by the other person as accusatory, which increases the chances of conflict.

Example: I believe I deserve compensation moving forward.

Your turn:

_____

_____

 ssert yourself.

Say what you want to happen clearly but not aggressively. This will help the other person understand you better.

Example: I would like overtime pay. Can you please arrange this?

Your turn:

_____

_____

 einforce your request.

Let the other person know that your request is important. So say how much you will appreciate it if you get what you want or need.

Example: I would really appreciate it if you arranged that. I will probably be even more productive because I know my extra hours are not taken for granted.

Your turn:

_____

_____

 indfulness.

Stay mindful of your words and emotions; stay focused and remain on topic no matter what the other person says.

Example: So, I hope you understand why I am requesting this. (Note: Aside from your words, ensure your body language is also mindful. For example, don't raise your voice and maintain a relaxed composure.)

Your turn:

_____

_____

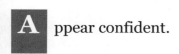 **A** ppear confident.

Show confidence through your words and body language. Do not apologize. Also, be consistent with your demeanor. For example, do not say what you want in a confident voice and then lower your voice as you continue your message.

Example: Sit or stand up straight, straighten your shoulders, maintain eye contact, and then say: I hope I am getting across to you because my stand on this won't change.

Your turn:

_____

_____

_____

_____

N egotiate.

Negotiate if the person you're talking to doesn't want to grant your request. This will allow you both to find an acceptable solution to the problem. You can offer a solution or ask the other person what they think should happen moving forward.

Example: I can do extra work this week and no further. But if you really want me to do extra hours next week, then I am willing to receive 75% overtime pay instead of full overtime pay. What do you think?

Your turn:

_____

_____

_____

_____

Worksheet: GIVE

GIVE aims to keep or improve our relationships with others *while* we try to get what we want from the interaction. Often, people say no to a request not because they don't agree with us but because of *how* we ask for it. (No one likes to be bullied into something or made to feel guilty if they don't agree with us!)

GIVE teaches us how to be effective in communicating what we want so that others are *induced* to grant our requests.

G	I	V	E
Gentle	**I**nterested	**V**alidate	**E**asy Manner
Be gentle. Do not offend the other person when communicating what you want. So that the other person doesn't feel assaulted, be kind and respectful.	**Act interested** in the other person by actively listening to them.	**Acknowledge** sentiments and emotions of the other person. Demonstrate that this discussion is not one-sided.	Adopt a **friendly and easy-going** manner. People will feel more at ease and will be more receptive to your requests when you have an engaging and pleasant attitude.
What do you want to <u>DO</u>?			
List 3 ways you can ask for something in a *gentle* way. *(e.g., use a friendly*	List 3 ways you can show that you are *interested* in what the other person is saying.	List 3 ways you can offer *validation* to others. *(e.g., repeat what*	List 3 ways to show that you are *easy to get along with*. *(e.g., smile, present*

G	I	V	E
voice)	(e.g., face the other person with your whole body; don't look at your phone)	the other person just said)	an "open" demeanor by not crossing your arms or legs)
1.	1.	1.	1.
2.	2.	2.	2.
3.	3.	3.	3.
What do you want to <u>SAY</u>?			
Example: I am angry about this situation but I can put that aside so we can arrive at a mutually-beneficial conclusion.	*Example: Will you give me some feedback? I am interested to get your viewpoint on this.*	*Example: You said you did not slam the door on me on purpose. So, does that mean you did not know I was behind you?*	*Example: I can see that we are both a bit flustered now. I don't want a fight, just clarification. Shall we discuss*

G	I	V	E
			this later?

DBT for Anger Management

You might be wondering if Dialectical Behavior Therapy is truly effective when dealing with anger issues. My personal experience is that it is very effective, and science agrees. Twenty-one (21) articles studying the effects of DBT on anger and aggressive behavior were peer-reviewed and found that DBT "shows a positive impact on the reduction of anger and aggressive behaviors".[11]

Acceptance and Change. The fact that you have this book in your hands says that you know you have anger issues and that you want to change because you want to lead a happier life. Well, congratulations! That's already the first step to Acceptance and Change in DBT!

DBT ACCEPT Skills

Anger is a strong emotion, and often we're reactive or impulsive to it. **Mindfulness** teaches us to be more in the moment and how to be fully aware of our surroundings and ourselves. Learning Wise Mind (page 25) in particular, teaches us to walk the middle path and always consult our emotions AND sensibleness (logic) before we do anything regarding our anger. Again, science agrees, as numerous studies have shown that Mindfulness is highly effective in reducing stress and anger and reducing aggressive behavior.[12,13,14]

Often, we lash out when angry because we cannot tolerate our anger. It consumes us, and we can't just bottle it up. **Distress Tolerance** teaches us the skills we need to deflect (not deny!) and tolerate our anger as it is happening, which is a good thing. Why? Because research has shown that high distress tolerance levels have a positive effect on our blood pressure during times of anger[15] and lowers our anger reactivity[16,17].

DBT <u>CHANGE</u> Skills

When we're angry, it doesn't help anyone (most of all ourselves) if we *stay angry*. **Emotion Regulation** skills teach us how to change unwanted emotions and how to manage extreme emotions so that we don't do or say something we will regret.

When we are angry, we are in a heightened sense of physiological arousal (e.g., blood pressure is elevated, body muscles are tensed, breathing exhilarates, etc.). As you can imagine, *staying* in this state is not good for you, so it is in your best interest to be able to regulate your emotions as quickly as you can. (*Plus, if you don't regulate your anger, chances are very high that you will react aggressively to other things and people around you, even if they have absolutely nothing to do with what prompted your initial anger.*)

Studies have shown that emotion regulation skills lead to "less anger experience" during times of anger[18] and make us more intentional and flexible (as opposed to impulsive) when responding to anger[19].

Interpersonal Effectiveness

When I look back at my anger issues, I realize that most of them were triggered by my family. This is not to assign blame; that's not part of DBT. I simply accept this as fact. So, for me, learning **Interpersonal Effectiveness** skills was crucial for successful anger management. After all, "anger is a common cause of strained negotiations".[20]

Even if your anger issues don't stem from people but more from situations, you'll find that most situations are often caused by humans, directly or indirectly. Again, this is not to assign blame. This is just to make you aware that, for the most part, dealing with your anger means dealing with people (yourself included!).

So, the better you are at interacting with others (interpersonal effectiveness), the more probable it is that you will avoid frustrating circumstances which can drive you to anger and aggressive behavior.

I hope that I have shared enough here to make you realize that DBT can be very useful when it comes to handling your anger issues. Don't worry; I'll share more DBT tools (exercises) with you in the succeeding pages. But for now, let's dive into ANGER itself.

A long time ago, a college friend, one of the first friends I truly had, asked me, *"Why are you always so angry?"* I found it very hard to explain, so I said, *"I JUST AM!"*.

To this, my friend replied, *"Well, you always seem angry and miserable, but that doesn't explain much, so don't blame me if I can't help you."*

The following chapter explains ANGER.

Believe me, it wasn't what I thought it was.

What is Anger?

*"Holding on to anger is like drinking poison
and expecting the other person to die." - Buddha*

 *Before you read up on what anger is all about, please take this
quick **Miller-Patton Anger Self-Assessment** exercise on
Appendix A (page 151).*

*Find out with just a few questions if you're handling your
anger well... or if anger is handling you.*

Anger 101

Anger is an emotion characterized by hatred toward someone, or something you
believe has purposefully wronged you.

Anger, in itself, serves a purpose. It can help you communicate negative feelings.
For example, if someone keeps crossing your boundaries, anger can prompt you
to speak up so that others learn to respect your wishes. However, anger is not
always about a person. You can be angry about certain situations. For example, if
you're angry about the fact that you need to drive half an hour to the nearest
grocery store, this may prompt you to find a solution to the problem, such as
moving to a different place that suites your lifestyle better. So, anger can lead to
better situations.

Anger itself does not get us in trouble; it is how we handle our anger that usually
does that.

When we are angry, it is hard to "think straight," so we tend to give in to impulse
and do something we will most likely regret later. This reaction is called the
amygdala hijack.

Amygdala Hijack

The *amygdala* is an almond-shaped form in the middle of the brain, and it forms part of the limbic system, which is a group of structures in the brain that help control our emotions (how we feel) and behavior (how we act).

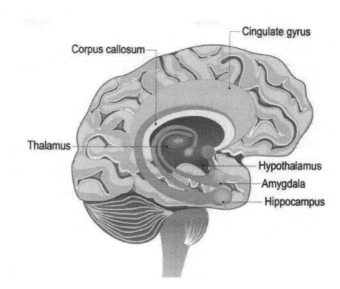

Under normal circumstances, the amygdala processes external frightening or threatening inputs and instructs our brains and bodies on how to respond. This is why the amygdala is strongly linked to our fight-or-flight response. In other words, when we detect a threat or danger, the amygdala produces hormones to get the body ready to either resist the threat or run from it.

The term **amygdala hijack** was first used by psychologist *Daniel Goleman* in his best-selling book "*Emotional Intelligence*" in 1995.[21] He describes it as **a strong emotional reaction that is out of proportion to the situation**.

Basically, the Reasonable Mind is bypassed, and Emotional Mind takes over. (No Wise Mind (page 25) here.) Later, when the information is processed by the part of your brain that lets you think (the prefrontal cortex), you realize that your reaction was completely disproportionate to the situation.

Physically, what happens is that when emotions (such as anger) run high, blood and oxygen flow to the amygdala (emotional hub) rather than the prefrontal cortex (thinking hub), reducing our ability to think and solve problems.

An amygdala hijack is useful in real life-threatening situations. For example, when you are crossing the street and a runaway car is hurtling toward you, reacting without thinking here can save your life.

The problem is that TODAY, we're faced with so many daily stressors that amygdala hijacks kick in easily, causing us to overreact. For example, if you're super busy trying to send out an already late report and your partner tries to talk to you, this may trigger the amygdala to take over, and you end up banging your keyboard and shouting at your partner.

Even though an amygdala hijack seems like a "natural reaction", it doesn't mean you need to give in to it. It may feel like everything is happening in mere seconds, but there's actually a process that your anger goes through.

The Anger Cycle

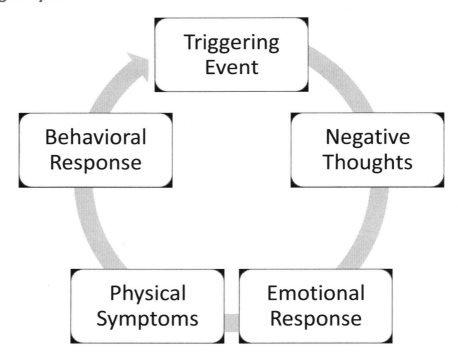

The **Triggering Event** is what caused your anger to begin with. Examples:

- A sibling who barged into your room and invaded your space.
- A co-worker who took credit for your hard work.
- Someone who cut you off while driving.

Negative Thoughts[†] or illogical thoughts fill your mind as a result of the triggering event. Examples:

- I absolutely HATE my sister/brother!
- [Colleague] is one lazy bastard who wants me to do all the work.
- The idiot who cut me off doesn't have a clue about driving rules and doesn't deserve to be on the road.

A negative **Emotional Response**[*] then arises as a result of your negative thoughts. Examples:

- **Shame/guilt.**

  I shouldn't hate my sister/brother. What's wrong with me?

- **Anxiety.**

  What is [colleague] going to do next? Give me more work? Ambush me on our next meeting? I am so stressed!

- **Rage.**

  That driver! I better not see that driver ever again because I don't know what I'll do!

As your negative thoughts and emotions consume you, **Physical Symptoms** begin to show. Examples:

[†] DBT founder Dr. Marsha Linehan believes that *Negative Thoughts* and *Emotional Response* are interchangeable. Sometimes, a triggering event prompts negative emotional responses, which then cause negative thoughts (and vice versa).

- Red face.
- Racing heartbeat.
- Clenched fists.
- Sweating.
- Clenched jaw and teeth.

Finally, your negative thoughts and emotions and their resulting physical symptoms become too much for you to bear, and a corresponding negative **Behavioral Response** ensues. Examples:

- You start arguing with your sibling.
- You explode and start yelling at your colleague.
- You drive fast and past the driver who cut you off. You get out of the car and start yelling and berating the other driver.

Actually, there's one more part of the cycle, the **Aftermath**.

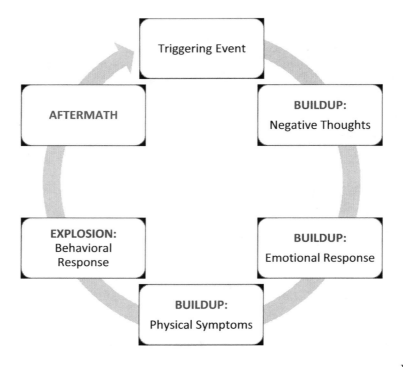

The **Aftermath** is dependent on your Behavioral Response. For example, say that you did react negatively to the situation; this may result in real-life negative consequences for you. Examples:

- Your argument with your sibling escalated to violence.
  Aftermath: Your parents ground you both, and you miss an important school event. A worse scenario is if one of you pushes the other (e.g., down the stairs), resulting in serious injury.
- Your argument with your colleague reaches the higher-ups.
  Aftermath: You get reprimanded or, worse, terminated.
- The driver who cut you off videotapes your outburst and calls the police.
  Aftermath: Jail time.

One thing I'd like to point out because this is what happened to me is that **Aftermath** comes one way or the other.

On many occasions, I kept my anger deep inside. I may not have always reacted aggressively or violently on the outside, but because I was not handling the Buildup phase of my anger effectively, the Aftermath for me was that it all contributed to my anxiety and depression mental health issues.

This is why I strongly advise applying DBT skills to address the Buildup phase of the anger cycle. Examples:

- Negative Thoughts -> Do the Grounding Technique exercise (page 29).
- Emotional Response -> Apply DBT Emotion Regulation skills (page 32).
- Physical Symptoms -> Engage in Mindful Breathing (page 24) or TIPP (page 31).

These are just some of the DBT skills that will help you get through the **Buildup** phase of anger, and as a result, you can avoid the **Explosion** and negative

Aftermath phases. (See <u>REAL LIFE Tools to Effectively Manage Your Anger</u> (page 87) for more DBT exercises.)

It also helps to understand how you express or unleash anger. Do you lash out? If you do, do you do so physically or verbally? Are you quick to anger or slow to anger? Is the target of your anger others or yourself? Let's go and find out.

The 10 Different Types of Anger

When you are angry, what *kind* of angry are you? You might be thinking, "*Does it matter*"? Yes, it does. If you know what kind of anger you're feeling at any given time, you'll be able to understand—and manage—it better.

1.   **Assertive Anger** uses frustration to bring about good or positive change. This is anger with a cause. You show your anger in ways that make things different around you without lashing out, screaming, or being aggressive with someone.

2.   **Behavioral Anger** is a manifestation of anger that is often aggressive. You feel overwhelmed by your feelings of anger that you lash out, often, at the person who made you angry, but at other times, you can keep your volatile emotions in and then lash out at others.

3.   **Chronic Anger** is a long-lasting, all-around resentment of people, frustration over situations, and anger at oneself.

4.   **Judgmental Anger** is a reaction to a slight that you believe others have done to you.

5. **Overwhelmed Anger** is a feeling of uncontrollable anger. It happens when you feel like you can't do anything about a situation or circumstance, which makes you feel hopeless and frustrated.

6. **Passive-Aggressive Anger** is a form of avoidance. This is when a person tries to stay away from any kind of conflict. This may mean having to bury any frustration or anger you might be feeling. However, it often slips out anyway, and you may engage in passive-aggressive comments, sarcasm, and even procrastination.

7. **Retaliatory Anger** is a natural reaction to being confronted or attacked by someone else. It is done to get back at someone for something they did wrong.

8. **Self-Abusive Anger** comes from feelings of shame. If you've been feeling hopeless, unworthy, embarrassed, or ashamed, you might keep those feelings inside and show your anger through negative self-talk, self-harm, drug use, or even eating disorders.

9. **Verbal Anger** is an aggressive and abusive type of anger. Usually, the angry person tries to hurt the target of their anger by shouting, screaming, ridiculing, blaming, or criticizing them.

10. **Volatile Anger**, also known as "sudden anger," is when a person gets angry over both big and small things that bother them. Since it is an explosive type of anger, it is often over as quickly as it starts. (This does not mean that there's no damage done by the outburst, though.)

Do you see yourself in any of the above? Please note that you don't necessarily have to fall into one anger type.

For me, I used to swing a lot between **Behavioral Anger**, **Chronic Anger** and **Passive-Aggressive Anger**. Later, I would find out that these were actually symptoms of my General Anxiety Disorder (GAD), but I didn't realize that my *gender* also had something to do with how I expressed my anger.

Male and Female Anger

It is a myth that men get angrier than women. Males may *display* their anger more often than females, but studies show that women get angry just as often and just as intensely as men.[22,23] It is also been discovered that *men feel less effective when pushed to control their anger*, while *women appear to be better able to control immediate instinctive reactions to rage*. Brain biology may have a hand here.

Brain Biology

The amygdala is the same size in both men and women, but a second part of the brain, the *orbital frontal cortex*, is smaller in men. Since this is the part of the brain that helps control aggressive impulses, it partly explains why men are less successful at keeping their tempers in check.

Societal Norms

Of course, let's not forget how society also plays a role in how men and women express anger. As children, when boys come home angry because someone teased them or fought with them, we don't ask how they feel or teach them how to process emotions. Most parents would say, "*toughen up*" or worse, "*get even!*". Sadly, this makes fighting look like the best way to express anger and solve problems. But we don't say the same things to little girls. In fact, we do the opposite. If little girls get upset or show anger, we tell them, "*that's unladylike*".

Yes, the above is a generalization, guilty of gender stereotyping and double standards, but it is also a fact. Luckily, times seem to be changing, but we cannot dismiss society's role in how men and women process and express anger. And these societal expectations do not stop in our youth.

As adults, an angry woman is seen as dramatic or emotional. One study even revealed that a woman who expresses anger is *"perceived as less competent, lower status, and having a lower salary"* than men and unemotional women.[24] As you can see, society generally encourages men to show anger and frowns on women who do.

But that's not fair, is it? Especially when we consider the following female biological differences.

Premenstrual Syndrome

Premenstrual syndrome (PMS) is a group of physical, emotional, and behavioral changes that start about a week before a female's menstrual cycle. About 75% of women globally experience PMS[25], and research shows that women with PMS experience anger more and have less control over their anger.[26]

Science has yet to explain why PMS is strong in some women and not in others. Still, it is clear that it is caused by the wildly changing levels of estrogen and progesterone hormones in a woman's body during the menstrual cycle. These hormone fluctuations influence *serotonin* levels, and low serotonin levels are linked to feelings of sadness, irritability, sleep issues, and food cravings.

Menopause

As women leave their reproductive years, *perimenopause* (the transition to menopause) kicks in. We've already learned above that *estrogen* and *progesterone* levels fluctuate during the menstrual cycle, resulting in low *serotonin* levels. During the perimenopause stage, these hormones are even more out of whack, resulting in intense emotions such as anger and rage.

As women transition into menopause, the roller-coaster of hormones can result in a lack of sleep, hot flashes, fatigue, low metabolism (resulting in weight gain), and others.

Menopause is not just a biological change. Often, these years signal many changes in a woman's life, such as kids leaving home, facing the realities of aging, waking up and realizing that you and your partner have grown apart, etc. All these changes, happening all at once, may be too much to handle and result in anxiety, depression, or anger.

So far, we've talked about WHAT anger is.

- Anger is an emotion characterized by hostility.
- Anger can make us react "out of proportion" to the situation (amygdala hijack).
- Anger may come on fast but there's a cycle that it goes through: trigger->buildup->explosion->aftermath.
- There are 10 different types of anger.
- There's a difference in how males and females experience and display anger.

However, everyone's "anger source" is different. One person's trigger may mean nothing to another. Different people also show their anger in different ways. So, in the next chapter, let's talk about YOUR ANGER.

Why Are You Angry?

By now, you have learned that anger is part of life and that it is one of the most primitive emotions we can experience as humans. However, anger can change how we think about risks.

A 2003 study has shown that anger makes us more impulsive and makes us think that bad things are less likely to happen.[27] In short, *if we don't take a moment to think, anger can make us reckless.* So let's take a moment to think. This chapter is all about you reflecting on your anger.

The Source of Your Anger

As mentioned before, anger is a reaction. To what? Usually, when people are angry, they immediately point to a person or a situation as the reason why they are angry. But neither is the real source of our anger, this is: the realization of our own impotence or powerlessness over a given situation. So, anger is really a coping mechanism.

If something unpleasant happened and we thought we could change the situation, we would have already done it, right? And in doing so, we wouldn't be frustrated or angry about it. However, since **we do not have control** and **cannot change the situation**, we are faced with the fact that **things are not as we want them to be,** and so **we get angry**.

It is also important to note that **anger is a secondary emotion**.[28] Researchers at *The Gottman Institute*[29], led by psychologists John and Julie

Gottman, created the *Anger Iceberg* to illustrate that anger is just the tip of the iceberg. Beneath the anger is a host of underlying thoughts, feelings, and emotions that cause it.[‡]

The Anger Iceberg

ANGER

hurt   humiliation
loneliness   shame
feeling inadequate
rejection
exhaustion
fear   sadness

Now that you know that anger is a response that usually stems from an underlying emotion, you can move on to exploring your triggers. These are the

---

[‡] The underlying reasons in this graphic are not all inclusive. Other thoughts, feelings and emotions (or a combination thereof), may be the source of your anger.

people, thoughts, feelings, and/or experiences that prompt or provoke your anger.

Clinical psychologist Nicole Lippman-Barlie, Ph.D. [30] encourages people to view anger as a communication tool. That is, *what is your anger trying to tell you?* Once you find the answer, you can prioritize that over your anger.

In my case, I figured out that my anger was not just a symptom of my anxiety disorder. Anger resulted from the *extreme loneliness* I have been feeling for years.

I spent most of my high school life alone. I did not have any friends even though the school I attended had over 5000 students. Every single day, I would eat lunch alone. And since there was no one to talk to, I'd soon be finished with lunch, so I would go to the library to hide or sleep. After school, I usually went to the arcade or internet cafe because I did not want to go home. If I did go home, I would stay in my room and play video games on my computer or N64. This was my way of escaping my own life.

Since I did not interact much with others, the few times I did usually ended in disaster. I would mumble my words, get all fidgety, and break into a sweat. This would then make me so upset and embarrassed that I would get very angry and find myself in a fit of rage.

In the beginning, I found it hard to accept. But eventually, I came to terms with the fact that I was *choosing* to lash out because it was harder to accept that no one liked me enough to be my friend.

Sadly, I did not know all this during my teen years. However, as an adult, knowing this enabled me to address my feelings of isolation and loneliness over my anger.

At this time, I was already aware of DBT, so I could apply the Interpersonal Effectiveness skills (page 40) I learned (see Worksheet: Finding Friends, page 41). Once I could address my loneliness, the anger I felt inside started to lose its grip on me.

So isolation and loneliness were my triggers or prompting events. These were the *underlying emotions* in my personal *Anger Iceberg*. What about you? Do you know what's causing your anger?

Following are three (3) worksheets to help you arrive at the REAL SOURCE of your anger. You don't have to do both Anger Triggers 1 (page 69) and Anger Triggers 2 (page 70). I have included two worksheets here because some prefer one type of exercise over the other. (Of course, you can also do both exercises if you want.)

Worksheet: Anger Triggers 1

Is your anger prompted by anything specific, or is it provoked by just about anything? Please think about each category below carefully. Is there a specific person or place that's always making you angry? Any specific thoughts or emotions making your blood boil? Write down your responses below.

Category	Your Replies
People *Example: mom, dad, my colleague Dave somehow always rubs me the wrong way, my ex*	
Places *Example: local café where I caught my partner cheating*	
Things *Example: pictures of my ex*	
Thoughts *Example: when I think that I am nowhere near my life goals*	
Emotions *Example: loneliness, sadness*	
Situations *Example: being ignored, when I binge-eat, being told I am wrong*	

Worksheet: Anger Triggers 2

If you find it hard to isolate what's prompting your anger *by category*, then perhaps the following worksheet is for you. Put a checkmark below **S** for sometimes, **A** for always, or **N** for never for each of the anger prompting events below to indicate how much of an anger trigger it is for you.

Potential Trigger	S Sometimes	A Always	N Never
When I am ignored			
When people don't keep promises			
When someone is crossing my boundaries			
When people don't understand me			
When others don't pull their weight			
When I am all alone			
When I am treated unfairly			
When somebody is mean to me			
When I am judged			

Potential Trigger	S Sometimes	A Always	N Never
When somebody doesn't think of my wants or needs			
When others are late			
When others are selfish			
When someone is trying to control me			
When people expect too much from me			
When I am disrespected			
When I am feeling threatened			
When someone embarrasses me			
When I don't know what's going on (facing the unknown)			
When I can't get help			
When I get rejected			

Potential Trigger	S Sometimes	A Always	N Never
When someone is lying			
When someone is insulting me			
When someone is giving me unsolicited advice			

Feel free to add any other potential trigger for you in the spaces below.

Worksheet: Anger Iceberg

Hopefully, after doing the **Anger Trigger** worksheets (pages 69 and 70) in the previous pages, you can fill out the underlying thoughts, emotions, and experiences causing your anger.

If you cannot fill out this worksheet now, that's okay. Go through the rest of this book if you need more clarity about your anger, and just come back to this worksheet when you're ready.

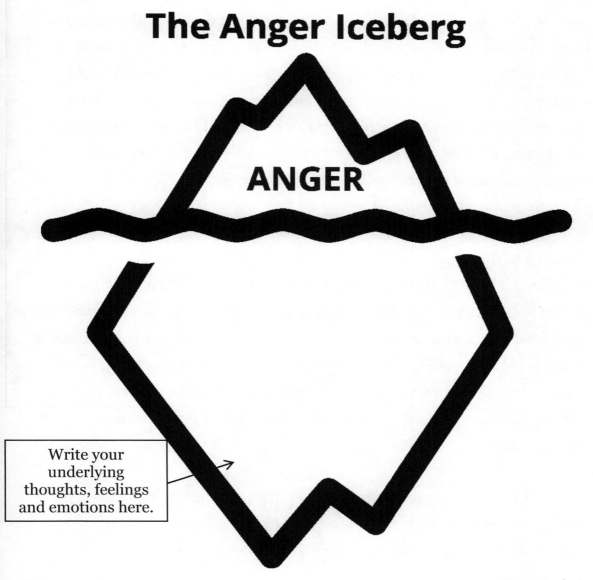

The Anger Iceberg

ANGER

Write your underlying thoughts, feelings and emotions here.

How Your Anger Grows

It is normal to feel as though your anger is intensifying over time. As we've learned in the previous section, anger results from our realization that things are not how we want them to be. If that continues for a considerable time, our anger flourishes due to *continuous unmet needs*.

Here's what my friend Ellen had to say about this:

"I am the eldest of three kids. When I was two years old, my twin brothers were born. From that moment on, the whole family doted on them. As a child, my wishes were always bypassed by whatever my younger brothers wanted. I started to "act out" at school (e.g., pulling a friend's hair, throwing books, scratching someone's arm, screaming, etc.). This prompted my parents to compare me even more to my twin brothers, who could do no wrong. By the time I was a teenager, my anger was uncontrollable. Everything at home triggered me. I just couldn't help but lash out at everything. Since no one paid any attention to me anyway, I ran away from home when I was 16.

For the first time, I felt free and felt like I could just be myself. I think it was the first time I felt any form of happiness. I supported myself by working two jobs during the day and attending night classes. Eventually, I found administrative work for a local construction company. However, after some time, I started to show burnout symptoms, and I could sense my anger issues returning, so I went to see a mental health professional. During this time, I learned that my anger stemmed from continuous unmet needs. What unmet needs? The need to be seen and valued for who I am.

Once I learned that my anger was a result of my feelings of being ignored, which, of course, stemmed from my childhood, I was able to address it by learning better ways of communicating what I needed."

So, if you feel your anger is growing or has been growing over the years, I encourage you to do the following.

1. **List the Top 3 things that anger you.** (**Tip**: Reflect on the previous section, The Source of Your Anger (page 65) and its worksheets.)

   Examples:

       a. *When my partner does not actively listen when I am talking.*

       b. *When my mom guilt trips me to visit every weekend.*

       c. *When my boss hands extra work on a Friday.*

   Your turn:

   _____

   _____

   _____

2. Identify the need that your anger may be expressing.

   Examples:

       a. *The need to be heard (NOT ignored).*

       b. *The need to own my weekends.*

       c. *The need to be considered; that my time is also valuable.*

   Your turn:

   _____

   _____

   _____

3. Develop a simple plan to address your unmet need(s).

   Important: *If you feel you're not ready to come up with a simple step-by-step plan at this stage to address your unmet needs, that's okay. Go through the rest of this book to learn more tools to handle your anger, and just return to this worksheet when you're ready.*

   Example situation: My partner does not actively listen when I am talking.

   (1) Have a sit-down with my partner (e.g., no kids, no phones, no distractions).

   (2) Tell them exactly how I feel (e.g., I feel completely ignored and unimportant when you're not giving me attention when I talk to you. I feel irrelevant.)

(3) Discuss how to make things better. (e.g., I understand you need to decompress when you just get home, so I'll do my best not to download on you then. But you need to tell me when is the best time to talk and how you intend to actively listen to me.)

Your turn:

_____

_____

_____

_____

_____

_____

_____

_____

_____

How Do You Express Your Anger?

Now that you have at least a clue as to the source of your anger let's discuss how you express your anger.

Most of the time, anger comes out in one of three ways:

- **External**. Other people can see a clear, outward sign of anger or aggression. This could include yelling, arguing, swearing, throwing or breaking things, having a temper tantrum (e.g., crying uncontrollably, pulling your hair, etc.), or being physically or verbally abusive to yourself or other people.

- **Internal**. This kind of anger is directed at yourself, not at other people or things, even if they caused your anger. This could include negative self-talk, self-denial of simple pleasures or even basic needs, self-harm, or self-isolation.

- **Passive**. This kind of anger is often shown in indirect and subtle ways, like ghosting, stonewalling or gaslighting someone, sulking, being sarcastic (depending on the situation), not helping on purpose or making snide remarks.

Why is it important to know how you express your anger?

As I keep mentioning in this book, anger is a valid emotion, and you shouldn't suppress or deny its existence. However, if you remember the quote at the start of this chapter, a right to be angry doesn't give you a right to be cruel—to others or yourself.

The three ways of showing anger above are all **destructive** ways of showing anger. Expressing your anger in any of these ways usually comes at a cost. (See The Costs of Your Anger, page 79)

So what's the alternative? <u>REAL LIFE Tools to Effectively Manage Your Anger</u> (page 87) will teach you how to effectively manage your anger (Mindfulness and Distress Tolerance) and how to express your anger in empowering, not destructive, ways (Emotion Regulation and Impersonal Effectiveness).

But before we dive into all of that, here's a quick recap of what we discussed in this chapter:

- Anger can make us reckless so it is important to understand the source of our anger.
- Anger is a coping mechanism. We find it hard to accept that things are not going our way and instead of understanding and fixing the situation, we react with anger.
- Anger is a secondary emotion (Anger Iceberg).
- To understand your anger, you must know your "prompting events" (anger triggers).
- Unaddressed anger is not moving on. It is an opportunity for anger to worsen over time.
- Anger is often expressed in one of three ways: external, internal, and passive.

The Costs of Your Anger

"For every minute you remain angry, you give up sixty seconds of peace of mind". - Ralph Waldo Emerson

Anger is a process that happens in both the body and the mind. As a result, anger can hurt your physical and mental health, especially if you express it in destructive ways. But these are not the only 'costs' to you. Uncontrolled, aggressive, explosive anger can also have serious financial, emotional, social and relationship costs.

Physical Costs of Anger

It is NOT healthy to be angry. As you have learned in <u>Anger 101 </u>(page 54), anger prompts the "fight or flight" response of the body. At this stage, adrenal glands release stress hormones such as adrenaline and cortisol into the body. The brain sends blood away from the gut and toward the muscles to get ready for any physical activity. The body's temperature increases, your heart rate, blood pressure, and breathing speed up too, and your skin begins to sweat.

As you can imagine, *chronic anger* can thus lead to *chronic stress*, leading to a host of health problems. Some of the short-term and long-term health issues that have been associated with uncontrolled anger are:

- migraines
- digestion problems
- insomnia
- high blood pressure (*hypertension*)
- high cholesterol
- skin problems

- strokes
- heart attacks

When I was growing up, whenever I got angry, and someone said, *"Careful. Think of your heart!"* I would get angrier because I thought they were making fun of me. Now I know that it is literally true!

Studies show that *anger increases your risk of getting different types of heart diseases, leading to death by up to five times the normal rate.* So, the angrier you are, the more likely you will get heart disease.[31,32,33]

Explosive anger can also lead to serious injury. Here's what my friend Norman had to say.

"My brother and I were the poster kids for 'sibling rivalry'. We did not support each other; we had to one-up each other. Our bodies are covered with cuts, scrapes, and stitches because we would get really physical when we got angry at each other. One day, I was up in the attic trying to find something when my brother followed suit and angrily accused me of trying to steal his skates. I saw red. I shoved him, and he fell down the stairs and broke his arm in three places. We were never "close," but that event made it clear that we didn't want each other in our lives moving forward."

Emotional Costs of Anger

As illustrated in the *Anger Iceberg* (page 73) anger is a secondary emotion. It could signify sadness, humiliation, fear, embarrassment, rejection, frustration, confusion, and other unhealthy emotions. If we stay angry, these unhealthy emotions will lead to emotional stress, affecting every aspect of our lives.

Destructive anger can also lead to a loss of self-esteem. Sometimes, we can't help it and let our anger out in explosive ways, which may feel good at the time, but it usually leads to guilt and shame. We end up feeling like this because we realize that our reaction was exaggerated, misdirected, or unjustified on some cognitive level. When this realization kicks in, we are not proud of ourselves, damaging our self-esteem.

There is also what we call "emotional aftershocks" resulting from anger outbursts. For example, say you couldn't control your anger and yell at your staff. You call them incompetent and, for good measure, rip and throw your keyboard across the room. Your staff feels humiliated. At best, you will no longer have their respect (a least not in the near future). At worst, your staff starts to lie, backstab and gossip about you at work. You're not a robot, so this begins to wear you down emotionally.

Also, consider this: if you let anger be the dominant emotion in your life, you reduce the amount of time you have to be happy. Anger, nurturing anger, and even trying to recover from anger all take time. Wouldn't you rather use that time to pursue things that make you happy?

Mental Costs of Anger

DBT teaches us that *choosing to stay in a negative state prolongs our own suffering*. That's certainly true in my experience. Isolation and loneliness were some of the root causes of my anger. Since I did not do anything to address these, I stayed angry—for years.

My chronic anger aggravated my anxiety disorder (GAD), and my passive-aggressive ways (i.e., I ruminate or think A LOT about my anger, but I don't always do something about it because I am always afraid I'll lose control and lash out) led to my depression.

Social Costs of Anger

No one likes to be with angry people. Just as nobody likes to be around a "downer", people also don't like being around someone who's always annoyed, irritated, or exasperated most of the time.

"Angry people" are seen as hard to deal with and exhausting. Many people also don't like to socialize with "angry people" because they don't want to be on the receiving end of that person's anger. Others still simply want to avoid any potential conflict or confrontation.

Regardless of the reason, the result for the person with anger problems is the same— *social ostracization*. Now, you may think, *"So what?"*

Humans are hard-wired with the need to belong.[34,35] On the emotional front, it hurts to be excluded, but you also miss a lot when you're not part of a group. Examples: a friendly neighbor who lends you a ladder so you can clean your top windows, a colleague who tells you about an opening you never even heard about, a cross-cultural friend who shares with you the joys of their food despite you never leaving the city you were born in, and so on.

Studies also show that a healthy social circle contributes to maintaining good physical and mental health.[36,37]

Financial Costs of Anger

Uncontrolled, problematic anger can have serious financial consequences. Studies show that anger problems may result in involuntary job loss[38] and make you handle your finances poorly[39].

For example, suppose you express your rage at your supervisor. In that case, you may be passed over for every chance of promotion, or worse, you may even face termination because you're not a "team player" or not "leadership material".

Anger may also lead to poor money decisions. For example, suppose you're angry because you're not financially where you want to be in life. In that case, you may act recklessly and spend money on lottery tickets, join quick-money schemes, and make poor investment choices, which may result in even more financial problems.

As for me, the financial costs of my anger came due to my inability to finish whatever it was I started. During my academic years, I kept switching majors because the minute things got difficult, I would get very angry and start blaming others, the environment, or life in general. Since things were not working in my favor, I figured I was studying the wrong thing, so I would switch to another major.

In total, I have studied in seven different programs and changed majors six times. The financial impact of that, not even considering the lost years when I could have been steadily working, is something I have never calculated. Why? I cannot alter the past, so I accept my choices. The best thing I can do is learn new behaviors so that I can change and not keep on making the same decisions. (See DBT Fundamentals: Acceptance and Change, page 17.)

Relationship Costs of Anger

Studies show that the people we know and love the most are the very ones we will most likely unleash our anger on, undeserved or not.[40] Perhaps, we do this because we feel "comfortable" with them and that at some level, no matter what we do, we hope we will be understood and forgiven. However, this is not always the case. Anger can leave long-lasting wounds on the people we care about, and it has the potential to destroy even the most "established" relationships.

In our rage, we may blurt out a loved one's secret, unjustly blame or accuse someone, verbally or physically hurt someone, and so on. These actions make it very difficult for the people we love to trust us again. It also makes them feel they cannot talk to us honestly because we might misunderstand and react angrily again. In the end, the result is the same: a breakdown in the relationship.

This is what my friend Monica had to say:

"When it comes to relationships, I am very insecure. No one would believe this because, on the outside, I am probably the most level-headed, non-dramatic, stick-to-the-facts woman you'll ever meet.

Greg and I got married after a year of dating, and he started to see that angry side of me; that side that would always accuse him of lying and cheating for no real reason and angrily threaten him with divorce. One time, about three years after being married, in a fit of rage, I violently threw a drinking glass over his head while he was sitting at the dinner table, the shattering glass echoing between us. Greg quietly got up, cleaned the mess, and went to bed. It made me angrier. I wanted to fight. He wanted to sleep?!

The following day, I was still seething with anger, and as per my usual script, I threatened him with a divorce. This time, he looked up at me and said, "I don't want that, but if you really do, I won't stop you." We broke up because, well, why would I back down? My anger was propelling me to take this path.

Years later, and after much therapy, I would understand the real reason for my uncontrollable anger: deep-seated abandonment issues. I never saw Greg again, but I heard he re-married and now has two beautiful girls. I would be lying if I said I never fantasize about what could have been."

In my anger journey, I can tell you that I have suffered all the different costs of anger mentioned in this chapter.

I have spent years suffering from insomnia, migraines, and a weak immune system (*physical costs*), an endless cycle of anger, shame, and regret (*emotional costs*), the worsening of my OCD and anxiety disorder, which led to depression (*mental costs*), the continuation of my isolation and loneliness (*social costs*), and going through six academic majors (*financial costs*).

As for *relationship costs,* my relationship with my family continued to be fragile at best and volatile at worst. Romantic relationships were not affected because, well, I did not have any.

I truly believe that had I continued down this path, my mental health problems, aggravated by my anger issues, would have continued, and at some point late in life, I would probably look back at an unhappy and unfulfilled life. Luckily, I reached for help, discovered DBT along the way, and changed the course of my life.

In the next chapter, I'll gladly share with you the DBT skills and tools I used to manage anger in real life. But before I do, here's a quick rundown of what we discussed in this chapter:

- Anger is a physical and mental process.
- Anger can wear down your body and cause various health problems.
- Anger that doesn't go away can cause emotional stress, which can affect every part of our lives.

- Anger can wear your mind down and lead to a number of mental health problems.
- Anger can lead to social ostracization.
- Anger can negatively affect your finances.
- When we're angry, we hurt the ones closest to us. As a result, anger can damage our most valued relationships.

REAL LIFE Tools to Effectively Manage Your Anger

"The boiling water that does not cool down only dries out!"
— Ernest Agyemang Yeboah

In Chapter 3 (page 65) you learned that we usually express our anger in destructive ways. In Chapter 4 (page 79) you learned that if you continue to express your anger destructively, you will eventually pay a very hefty price for it. As such, learning healthy and empowering ways to manage and express your anger is crucial. But before you can do that, you must understand the link between anger and vulnerability.

Anger and Vulnerability

As you have learned, anger is our response when we sense a threat, perceive that someone has done us wrong, or experience any form of injustice or unfairness. In many ways, anger keeps us "safe". How? Well, if we focus on anger itself, then we don't need to dig deep and find out WHY we are angry. Often, understanding the WHY is more painful and harder to accept.

As I have previously shared with you, I stayed angry for years because I didn't want to know why I was so alone and isolated in this world. I already had OCD and anxiety disorders, so I don't think I could have dealt with the physical and emotional pain of not being loved. I know that's not true today, but back then, I thought I only had two options: be angry or accept that no one cares about me. I chose anger.

The anger made me feel that I had some semblance of control in my life. Being angry was better than being invisible. But here's the bottom line: anger wasn't better. It did not solve anything, and I was just getting more and more miserable!

With professional help, I learned that letting myself *feel vulnerable* is the first step to healing and stopping my anger from controlling my life. Believe me; I know this is not easy; to "not be angry" means to experience fear.

Remember, this is how it is in a nutshell: when we sense threat or danger, wrongdoing, unfairness, or injustice, the amygdala is triggered. The amygdala is the part of our brain that controls our emotions (*how we feel*) and behavior (*how we act*). So, what are we left with if we don't go into anger? Fear or anxiety, right? And NO ONE likes feeling this vulnerable.

I know this all sounds scary, but I have learned that vulnerability doesn't mean giving up control and letting other people hurt me. It is about being honest and open with myself about the things that hurt me or cause me sadness.

Once I gave myself permission to feel vulnerability, I started to understand my anger, how to effectively deal with it when it happened, and how to get rid of the things that made me angry in the first place. And guess what? Since I fixed what was causing my anger, I was no longer angry.

Top 8 Tips to Be More Vulnerable

Vulnerability or emotional exposure is not a weakness. In fact, it takes a lot of strength and courage to allow yourself to feel vulnerable. Understandably, years of hiding your true self and denying your wants and needs mean that feeling vulnerable takes some getting used to. So, the following are some tips to help you be okay with feeling vulnerable.

 # 1. Discover yourself and learn to love the person you uncover at the end of that journey. We spend so much time twisting and turning ourselves into the people others expect to see that we lose who we really are in the process. So my advice is to take the time to get to know yourself.

Here's what my friend Kara had to say:

"Everyone was an over achiever in my family. You can say that I was considered the weakest link. Overtime, I just absorbed this belief. I wouldn't share my thoughts because it probably wouldn't be as great as what others would say. I wouldn't go against anyone because, well, what did I know? I developed the mindset that people are always "better" than me.

Unsurprisingly, as an adult, I suffered from very low self-esteem, which manifested into self-abusive anger. During therapy, I realized that as much I loved my family, I needed to get away from them. I took a job that took me to India. Despite everyone in my life telling me that I shouldn't do it and that I was making a big mistake, I went ahead with it. I was at a place where I just wanted to be on my own, and it was the best decision I had ever made.

Contrary to my own belief, I was not weak at all. I was strong and very capable of finding solutions to problems on my own. I did discover that I had this tendency to hide myself, my real thoughts, and my real feelings for fear of being reprimanded or overstepping someone, so I still have work to do. But I am just so glad that I had the courage to take the step to discover me."

 # 2. Be honest. No one is perfect, and part of being vulnerable is knowing your weaknesses, your "less-than-lovable" sides, and acknowledging and admitting mistakes you have made. It is also about learning to communicate what you need from others, including your expectations and boundaries. (**Tip**: If you need help establishing boundaries, see <u>How to Set Boundaries</u> on page 128.)

3. **Stop seeking the approval of others.** Be 100% okay with who you are, regardless of what others think. Vulnerability is often associated with weakness because it exposes us to other people's opinions and judgments. But if we stop valuing other people's opinions about us above our own, then we will be free to be who we want to be without fear.

In my teens, I was always trying to be friends with everyone. Please note that a healthy sense of *belongingness* is good for our well-being.[41] However, overdoing this is not good because this is when you will lose yourself. This is what happened to me.

I was always seeking the approval of others; what they thought of me was more important than what I thought of myself. This meant I was always trying to change myself into the person I thought other people wanted me to be. In the end, the "friendship" I was looking for never happened, and I'd go back to feeling anxious, depressed, and angry.

Today, whenever I look back, I realize that I shouldn't have spent so much time and effort caring about what others thought of me. For one, I hardly kept in touch with any of them. Most importantly, I should have paid more attention to myself, learning to know and love myself.

4. **Learn how to say "sorry".** I have learned that my anger issues were very much connected to my ego. In the past, I would much rather be enraged than say sorry because that meant (1) I did something wrong and (2) I needed to take responsibility for my actions.

Saying sorry is something my whole family struggles with. You see, in the Chinese culture, saving face and not looking bad is very important so it's rare for anyone in my family to apologize or admit fault. This was just not "normal" to me.

I also thought that apologizing showed people that I had low self-esteem. I had it backward.

Over the years, I have come to the conclusion that the most secure, confident people have no qualms apologizing at all. They're 100% okay with admitting mistakes and saying sorry precisely because they have great self-esteem.

A friend also shared something very powerful with me. She said, *"Apologizing doesn't always mean admitting wrongdoing. Even if you didn't do anything wrong, can't you merely be sorry that your actions caused someone else's feelings to be hurt?"*

Further, saying sorry, even if you did not do anything wrong, opens the lines of communication, enabling you to build trust and reconnect with the person who got hurt.

5. **Take chances.** They say that a human being's greatest fear in life is the unknown. If we are unsure of the outcome, there's a big chance of loss or failure. But we forget there's also an equal possibility for gain and success. So learn to take chances. Sure, the results may not be what you thought they would be—they could be better.

After I graduated from university, I had the opportunity to move to Korea and teach English in a public school. This was a VERY big move for me; many changes would happen. Ultimately, I decided to take the chance, and it was the best decision of my life! I grew a lot as a person and ended up staying in Korea for three years.

So if ever you're presented with an opportunity for change (e.g., striking up a conversation with someone you like, asking for a raise, raising your hand to lead a team, etc.), take the chance. You never know when such an opportunity will present again.

6. **Write down your fears.** Find a safe and quiet space, and then write down all your fears. They don't need to be in any order; just let all those fears tumble out of you. Keep the list and revisit it in a day or two. When you read them again, take a really good look at them. This will give you a better idea of how significant your fears are as a result.

Examples:
I'm afraid my relationship won't last.
I'm afraid of speaking in front of a group.
I'm afraid to reconcile with my parents.

After some time, revisit these fears and really deliberate on them. (**Tip**: Use Wise Mind, page 25.)

For example: *I'm afraid my relationship won't last.* Instead of fearing what MAY happen, why not focus on what IS happening. How long are you in the relationship? How has this relationship helped you and your partner develop, individually and as a couple? What other great ways can you grow this relationship?

 # 7. Get comfortable with sharing personal information. We are NOT in the habit of sharing too much about ourselves because we fear many things: rejection, disappointment, abandonment, and so many other insecurities. But if you want to be more comfortable with being vulnerable, you have to learn to share more about your real self. Start with simple guilty pleasures like admitting to like a particular reality TV show, having a fondness for 80's pop songs, checking celebrity gossip sites from time to time, and so on.

 # 8. Don't be afraid to ask for help. It is easy to isolate yourself from others when you're hurting or feeling unsure. However, a crucial component of vulnerability is admitting to loved ones that you need them, even if it is just to listen.

How Does Vulnerability Help Me With My Anger?

"You can't get to courage without walking through vulnerability." – Brené Brown

---

Anger is a shield. We use it to protect ourselves from feeling and experiencing deep physical, mental, and emotional pain. At this stage, your anger is probably an "automatic response," so it is hard to just "get on and deal with it." However, suppose you're comfortable with feeling vulnerable. In that case, you'll be much more open and ready to adopt the DBT skills and exercises in the next pages.

Worksheet: Vulnerability List

Getting comfortable with vulnerability is not a switch you can just turn "on." You need to get used to it. Following are a few things you can do to practice feeling vulnerable. Write down the date you did each one and your thoughts about them.

Notes:

- You don't need to do the items in any order. Just do the ones you're comfortable doing for now.
- Feel free to do any activity more than once.
- Not all of them may apply to you, so feel free to skip a few and add your ideas to the list.

Activity	Date	Thoughts
Example: *Greet a complete stranger.*	*Aug. 1*	*I was uncomfortable, but the experience was NOT as bad as I thought it would be.*
Example: *Greet a complete stranger.*	*Aug. 2*	*I greeted them, but the person did not greet me back. First, I was annoyed because I put myself out there, but I am OKAY with it. I realized I don't control other people's actions, only my own.*
Greet a complete stranger.		
Ask for feedback.		
Say sorry to someone.		
Ask someone for help.		

Activity	Date	Thoughts
Make an unpopular suggestion.		
Share an unpopular opinion.		
Go somewhere you know you'll need to wait. (e.g., a popular coffee shop, grocery store during peak hours, etc.) *Note: The vulnerability part here is exposing yourself to feelings of frustration (due to impatience). IF you're feeling overwhelmed and feel yourself getting angry, leave the situation.*		
Join friends on a night out knowing there's a big chance of changes in plans during the night.		
Take a cooking class. *Note: Actually, you can take any class you want. The vulnerability part here is knowing you're not in control of the situation. You're deliberately surrounding control to the class teacher. You are here to follow.*		
For singles:		

Activity	Date	Thoughts
Go on a blind date.		
For married couples: **Schedule a time to talk to your partner about anything that's bothering you or them.** *Note: The vulnerability part here is opening yourself to your partner. Avoid interrupting if they have something to say that hurts or offends you. Just hear them out and wait for your turn to say anything. IF you're feeling overwhelmed and feel yourself getting angry, take a break. DO NOT respond in anger.*		
Do something you know you're not good at.		
Share one personal thing with someone you trust.		
Call or reach out to someone you have lost touch with.		
Call out someone constantly breaking your boundaries.		
Tell someone you care.		
Say NO to someone.		

Activity	Date	Thoughts
Feel free to add more activities to the extra rows below.		

Mindfulness Skills for Anger Management

When we are angry, it feels like everything is happening so fast. Amygdala hijack (page 55) kicks in, and before we know it, we say or do something we usually regret. Sometimes, though, anger doesn't come over us quickly; it can be a feeling that simmers just beneath the surface. Still, anger has the power to dominate, whether it rises suddenly in a flaming burst or burns quietly over time. And when that happens, we either lash out or internalize the feeling, neither of which is good.

Mindfulness helps calm the amygdala, the part of the brain that is linked to fear and emotion. In fact, a 2013 study revealed that after eight weeks of practicing mindfulness, the amygdala seemed to shrink. As the amygdala shrank, the pre-frontal cortex, which is linked to higher-order brain functions like being aware, focusing, and making decisions, got thicker.[42]

In short, mindfulness weakens the part of the brain that focuses on emotions and strengthens the part that helps us think logically and make decisions. By practicing mindfulness, or being in the moment, we teach ourselves to be less controlled by strong emotions like anger.

Worksheet: Mindful Body Scanning (Anger Observation)

This Mindfulness exercise will help calm your nerves, focus your thoughts, and center your being when feeling angry.

1. Sit or lie down, whatever is most comfortable for you. Close your eyes.

2. Breathe in deeply for a count of four (4), and then exhale for a count of four (4). Do this two (2) more times. (Three rounds in total).

3. Starting with the top of your head, become aware of your scalp. Is it feeling tight because of your anger? If so, take a deep breath in and as you exhale, deliberately relax your head. If it helps, shake your head gently from side to side. Imagine your scalp loosening because of this.

4. Next, move on to your forehead. Is it *scrunched* because of your anger? If so, take a deep breath in and as you exhale, deliberately relax your forehead. Release all those angry lines.

5. Next, move on to your eyebrows. Is one arched more than the other because of your anger? If so, take a deep breath in and as you exhale, deliberately relax your eyebrows. Release all that tension.

6. Next, move on to your cheekbones. Are they tight and elevated because of your anger? If so, breathe in and as you breathe out, relax your cheeks.

7. Continue down until you've covered your whole body.

After you have done this exercise a couple of times, you'll gain knowledge about how your body physically reacts to anger. For example, not everybody scrunches their forehead and brings their eyebrows together when angry.

For me, my top physical anger expressions are: (1) clenched jaw, (2) tight shoulders, and (3) clenched fists. I never knew this about myself until I started doing the above exercise whenever I felt angry. When I learned this about myself, I could calm down faster by zeroing on these three body parts. Here's what I do:

1. Clenched jaw? I take a deep breath in, and as I exhale, I force myself to smile a bit. I take a deep breath in again, and as I exhale, I smile a bit wider, and so on.
2. Tight shoulders? I take a deep breath in, and as I exhale, I force myself to relax my shoulders. I take a deep breath in again, and as I exhale, I slowly round my shoulders.
3. Clenched fists? I take a deep breath in, and as I exhale, I open my hands wide. I take a deep breath in again, gently closing my fists as I do so, and as I exhale, I open my hands wide.

There's no rule about how many 'rounds' of breathing you need to do. It all depends on how angry you are at the moment and how fast you can calm down. As always, practice makes progress. Before you know it, this will all become a habit for you.

Worksheet: Mindfully Angry (Anger Description)

Sometimes, all it takes to deal with anger is simply to recognize it. Yes, this is hard to do when you're really angry, but doing so lessens the effect of your anger. If we fight, hide, or deny our anger because we don't like how it makes us feel, our anxiety and negative feelings about the situation tend to worsen. As what DBT teaches us, this just prolongs our suffering (from anger).

1. Sit or lie down, whatever is most comfortable for you. Close your eyes.§

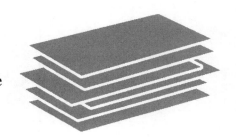

2. Imagine a stack of paper next to you. In simple words, describe your anger. Write down every word that comes to your head. It can be an emotion, a person, a place, an activity, a color, anything!

For example, on a piece of paper, imagine writing the word "**red**" or the phrase "**seeing red**." Mentally take that piece of paper, crumple into a ball and throw it in your imaginary waste basket.

It is important that you do this exercise non-judgmentally. Just describe the anger, don't evaluate it. Don't stay on it either (ruminate). Write and release. Write and release. Write and release.

When you write down your anger descriptors, you're accepting your current state. When you release them, you're helping yourself calm down.

---

§ If you prefer, make this a physical exercise rather than a mental one. That is, grab a stack of paper, a pen and a place a wastebasket near you.

Distress Tolerance Skills for Anger Management

Anger is such a powerful, overwhelming emotion. So much so that we cannot help ourselves from lashing out, internally or externally. But basically, we do this because we cannot tolerate our distress.

Remember the Anger Cycle (page 56)?

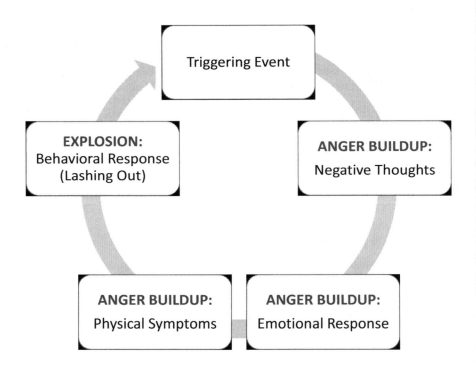

But what if you can tolerate that emotional distress (Anger Buildup)? If you're able to do that, then you can prevent the next process (Explosion), right?

The following DBT Distress Tolerance exercises will help you build the skills you need so that your (anger) cup never flows over.

Worksheet: Radical Acceptance

Radical Acceptance is based on the idea that *we suffer because we are attached to our anger, not because anger is bad in and of itself.* By getting angry and telling yourself that this situation "should not be happening," you miss the point that the situation is already happening, with or without you, with or without your consent.

This does NOT mean that you give up and give in. Instead, Radical Acceptance means that you know that denying your anger-related thoughts and feelings won't change the situation. If you fight, ignore or deny anger, you get stuck in thoughts like, *"Life is so unfair!", "Why me?!", "I don't deserve this!", "this is NOT right!"*

Remember too that Radical Acceptance is NOT the same as approval or consent. Instead, it means accepting with your whole mind, body, and spirit that you cannot change the present situation, even if you don't like it. By radically accepting the things you cannot change, you avoid getting stuck in anger.

I'll be the first to admit that learning to accept something we don't like is very difficult. Whenever I got frustrated, it was very hard for me to radically accept the situation when every fiber of my being was trying to go to my default mode: *anger.*

However, humans are not born with anger. Yes, we have the potential to feel every emotion on the planet, including anger, but anger styles and anger responses are all learned.[43] So, this means that we can unlearn it.

It takes time to unlearn the old and learn the new, but it is not impossible. The following worksheet will help you learn how to apply Radical Acceptance when you're angry.

1. **OBSERVE.** Notice HOW you are fighting reality or questioning it.

   Example: Oh no, this shouldn't be happening! (This is denying the situation).

   Your turn: *(List down the ways you may be ignoring, fighting, or denying your anger.)*

   _____

   _____

   _____

2. **REMEMBER.** Remind yourself that the current situation (reality) is the way it is and cannot be changed.

   Example: I don't like it, but it is what it is.

   Your turn: *(Write down your own anger acceptance statement.)*

   _____

   _____

   _____

3. **RATIONALIZE.** Remind yourself that there are reasons behind this current situation. Recognize that past events have led to this exact moment. It did not just happen; there are reasons why things happened this way.

   Example:

   Situation: I am furious at [colleague] for stealing my marketing idea.

   Possible Reason 1: I let [colleague] pass his workload to me before, so this probably let them think they can always get away with things like this.

   Possible Reason 2: When [boss] asked for ideas, I did not speak up.

   Your turn: *(Write down your reasons.)*

   _____

   _____

   _____

   _____

   _____

4. ACCEPT. Practice acceptance of the situation involving your whole being.

Examples:

Accepting with my mind: I am okay. I accept this. It is all good.

Accepting with my body: do <u>Body Scanning</u>

Your turn:

_____

_____

_____

5. PRACTICE OPPOSITE ACTION. List down everything that you would do, assuming that you have indeed radically accepted the situation.

Example:

Situation: I was furious at [colleague] for stealing my marketing idea.

(1) I did Body Scanning, so I am physically relaxed now. I will NOT have an angry demeanor when I meet [colleague].

(2) When I meet [colleague], I will not replay the meeting in my mind.

Your turn:

_____

_____

_____

_____

_____

_____

6. COPE AHEAD. Close your eyes and imagine radically accepting something you do not want to. Visualize acceptance anyway. That is, play in your mind what you're going to do.

Example:

Situation: I find it very hard to accept reading the new marketing materials because they will have [colleague]'s name as the author.

Visualizing acceptance:

(1) When I receive the new marketing materials, I will read them without resentment. I will treat them just like any marketing material in the company.

Your turn:

_____

_____

_____

_____

_____

7. ATTEND. Pay attention to your physical reactions while you consider what you need to accept.

Example: While visualizing acceptance, I can feel myself starting to clench my fists. I should do some deep breathing and open my hands wide each time I exhale.

Your turn:

_____

_____

_____

_____

_____

8. ALLOW. Give yourself permission to feel disappointed, upset, or grieve.

Example:

Situation: I am furious at [colleague] for stealing my marketing idea.

Allow: I am feeling really sad about the missed opportunity.

Your turn:

_____

_____

_____

9. ACKNOWLEDGE. Recognize that even in the face of hardship, life is still worth living!

Example:

Situation: I am furious at [colleague] for stealing my marketing idea.

Acknowledge: I'll get through this. Another opportunity will present itself, and next time, I'll have an even better idea to share.

Your turn:

_____

_____

_____

10. PROS & CONS. Whenever you're unable to radically accept a situation, chances are you'll feel an overwhelming need (urge) to act on your anger. Use the **Pros & Cons** table below to help you fight your urge.

Pros & Cons is about considering the positive and negative aspects of acting and not acting on your anger. The goal is for you to see that tolerating your anger is better than acting on your anger impulses.

Example:

Situation: [Colleague] stole my marketing idea and presented it as theirs.

Urge: Lash out.

Your turn:

Your Situation:

_____

Your Urge:

_____

	Acting on Your Urge	Resisting Your Urge
PROS	*Example:* *I'll feel some relief.*	*Example:* *I won't regret anything tomorrow.*
CONS	*Example:* *I might physically harm someone.* *My boss may frown at my "short-temper."*	*Example:* *I might internalize my anger.*

Worksheet: STOP

Often, when we are angry, we don't have time to think. <u>Mindfulness</u> (page 22) and <u>Radical Acceptance</u> (page 103) skills are the PAUSE buttons you can apply to prevent lashing out. Sometimes, though, the desire to act on your anger impulses (urges) is so strong that you can barely contain yourself. In this scenario, adopt the **STOP** skill below. It will help prevent you from acting on impulse and make a stressful or hard situation even worse.

 top.

Stop! Freeze. Don't move a muscle.

Physically freezing for a moment prevents you from acting impulsively (which is acting in Emotion Mind).

Example: A co-worker has taken credit for work you've done, and you have this insane urge to punch them in the face. Instead of doing so, FREEZE in your tracks.

 ake a step back.

Take a physical and mental step back from the situation. Take a deep breath and continue to do so for as long as necessary until you are in control. Remember this: we hardly ever need to make a split-second decision about anything, so give yourself time to think before you act.

Example: You're very angry at your partner for volunteering YOUR time this weekend to a cause you don't even believe in. Before you say or do something you'll regret, FREEZE and then TAKE A PHYSICAL STEP BACK. Of course, don't just leave. That will lead to even more misunderstandings. Say to your partner, "Wait, I am not okay with what you did. I need a moment," and then leave the room.

bserve.

Take note of what is going on within you and around you. Do this one-mindfully and non-judgmentally. That is, literally observe things as if you're making a list.

Example of observing yourself: I am sitting. My face feels hot. My breathing is ragged.*
Example of observing your surroundings: There's a ball on the floor. There's a half-filled water glass on the table. My partner is looking at me.

* Since you notice that your breathing is ragged. Make a deliberate choice to practice Mindful Breathing (page 24).

What are you observing?

_____

_____

_____

roceed mindfully.

You've taken a break from your emotions, and now it is time to proceed mindfully. Enter Wise Mind (page 25) and ask yourself, *"What do I want to happen?"*, *"How do I make this situation better?"*, *"How do I honor my feelings AND be reasonable about this situation?"*

Example: Okay, I don't want to go, but my partner says it is only for an hour. I can deal with that. But I need to tell them that (1) moving forward, they should respect MY time, so they need to ask me first before if I am okay with whatever they're planning, and that (2) since I am compromising, I'll hold to that one hour, and if it goes further, my partner will understand and NOT get angry if I leave.

What do you want to do to proceed mindfully?

_____

_____

_____

Worksheet: ACCEPTS

Distraction is one of the best ways you can ride out your anger. The following DBT exercise is called **ACCEPTS**. It is a great way to build your frustration tolerance levels because it can give you the space you need to process your anger. It helps you divert your attention, which helps calm your emotions down.

 ctivities.

Make a list of stimulating and attention-demanding activities that you enjoy doing. The goal is to draw yourself completely into doing something fun so that you don't spend any mental, physical, or emotional resources on your anger.

Examples: solve a puzzle, engage in coloring by number by getting a coloring book or downloading an app like Color by Number for Adults, follow a new exercise routine on YouTube

Your turn:

_____

_____

_____

 ontributing.

Turn your attention to others' needs. Contributing will make you feel good and take your mind off your own problems.

Examples: de-clutter and donate old clothes, volunteer to clear a neighbor's front yard, check your kitchen cabinets and find at least 10 food items to donate, etc.

Your turn:

_____

_____

_____

C omparisons.

Recall an infuriating situation in the past that's worse than your current frustration.

Example: I got so frustrated with my brother not answering my text messages that I sent a very angry message listing down all the things he owed me and called him ungrateful. Our relationship has never been the same since.

Your turn:

_____

_____

_____

E motions.

Do something completely opposite to how you feel. So think about what you would normally do when you're angry and then deliberately do the contrary.

Examples:

I want to SCREAM! (Opposite: Be quiet and meditate.)

I want to clench my jaw and fists. (Opposite: Smile and open your hands wide.)

Your turn:

_____

_____

_____

P ush away.

Actively push your anger away. Select your desired action from the list below. Feel free to include extra choices as well.

- ☐ Go somewhere where you can be alone and then, in your loudest voice, say, **STOP! GO AWAY!**
- ☐ Write down your "anger words" (e.g., *pissed, furious, red, boiling*, etc.) on a piece of paper, and then let them go by burning the paper. (Alternatively, see Mindfully Angry on page 101.)
- ☐ Take a stroll. Pick up a leaf. Imagine that the leaf represents your anger, and then let it go and watch it drift away from you. If this is too gentle for you, pick up a stone. Imagine it representing your anger, and then throw it as hard and as far away from you as you can.
- ☐ Others:

_____

_____

_____

T houghts.

Transport yourself to a happy time in your life (happy thoughts).

Examples: watch a feel-good movie; look at a picture of a loved one, relive a surprise that family or friends did for you

Your turn:

_____

_____

Sensations.

Distract your angry thoughts and feelings by subjecting yourself to different physical sensations. Select what you want to do below, and feel free to include extra choices as well.

- ☐ Suck on a lemon wedge.
- ☐ Eat a few pieces of really hot (spicy) spicy chips.
- ☐ Hold ice cubes.
- ☐ Chew intensely sour gum.
- ☐ In winter, walk out in the cold.
- ☐ Others:

_____

_____

_____

Emotion Regulation Skills for Anger Management

Anger can be long-lasting. Some people get angry quickly, they lash out and explode, and then they are done. For others, like me, anger stays for days on end.

One of the reasons anger is so hard to regulate is because it IS a powerful emotion. But then again, it is a power we give. By not regulating anger and moving forward, we give it the fuel it needs to stay and dominate our lives.

Emotion Regulation is all about influencing the anger we have, when we have it, how we experience it, and how we express it. It is that we are controlling anger instead of the other way around.

The DBT exercises below will help you up-regulate positive emotions, which in turn down-regulate our susceptibility to anger. The goal is simple: regulate your anger so that you feel less angry.

Worksheet: BPE

A happy person is not easily angered. **BPE** stands for **B**uild **P**ositive **E**xperiences, and it is an exercise designed to increase positive emotions in your life, thereby reducing your capacity for anger and other negative emotions.

Build Positive Experiences I

Write down 10 experiences that make you instantly happy. These are positive events that make you feel better while doing them or immediately thereafter.

 # 1. Example: walking my dog

 # 2. Example: tending to my herb garden

 # 3. Example: meditating

4.

5.

6.

7.

8.

9.

10.

Build Positive Experiences II

Choose one experience from the list above, and then resolve to do it every day. What you decide to do and how long you wish to do it is not important. The goal is to do it EVERY SINGLE DAY. (Daily happy habits!)

Example: meditating

I will <u>meditate</u> every day for <u>30 minutes in the morning</u>.

Your turn:

I choose: _____

I will _____ every day for _____.

Build Positive Experiences III

Write down 10 experiences that have the potential to give you long-lasting happiness. These are positive events that you may need to plan for, but when achieved, their positive impact on your life is long-term.

1. *Example: take a cooking class*

2. *Example: get a gym membership*

3. *Example: go on a weekend getaway alone*

4.

5.

6.

7.

8.

9.

10.

Worksheet: PLEASE

Your physical health has a direct impact on your emotional health and vice versa.[44] So, to create positive emotional change, it is crucial to take care of your body too.

This DBT exercise emphasizes the importance of taking care of our physical health because an unhealthy body makes it difficult for us to manage our emotions.

PL Physical Illness

Don't wait to see a doctor and take any prescribed drugs if you're feeling physically sick. It is also advisable to reach out to someone (e.g., a friend, a family member, a neighbor, etc.) so that you are not by yourself through this time. If you don't want to consult a physician or are physically unable to do so, then, by all means, pursue a holistic approach to wellness. The idea is to GET HELP so that your illness doesn't worsen.

When was the last time you were physically ill?

_____

Did you see a doctor? Y / N
Why or why not?

_____

_____

E Balanced Eating

Make sure you're consuming a nutritious, balanced diet. Avoid anything that comes from a bag or a jar (processed food). As much as possible, eat food in its natural form. For example, if you want to put strawberry jam on your toast, which is high in sugar, put real strawberries instead.

Below is a quick, **7-day Healthy Swaps** log. It is important to note that the objective here is NOT to lose weight. The table below is simply a tool you can use to make you aware of any unhealthy food choices you may be making today and to swap them for healthier ones.

If you're already doing this, great! I encourage you to move on to more detailed food journaling using apps like MyFitnessPal.

Note: Please always consult your doctor or a nutritionist before making any drastic food changes in your diet.

7-Day Healthy Swaps		
Day	**Current Food Choice**	**Swap**
Monday	*Example: white bread*	*Example: wholegrain bread*
Tuesday		
Wednesday		
Thursday		
Friday		
Saturday		
Sunday		

A Avoid Unhealthy Substances

Consuming unhealthy substances such as caffeine, alcohol, and prohibited drugs can exacerbate your anger, so avoid taking them. Instead, consume water or lemon water, green tea, healthy smoothies, etc.

S Sleep

Adults need seven (7) or more hours of quality sleep each night.[45] If you don't, you'll have low energy levels, which makes you more likely to give into anger and display aggressive behaviors.[46]

To check if you're getting enough sleep, try this **7-Day Sleep Log**. Just jot down the time you sleep and the time you wake up and calculate your total sleep hours.

7-Day Sleep Log			
Date	**Sleep Time**	**Wake Time**	**Total Sleep Hours**
Monday	*Example:* 11:30 PM	*Example:* 6:00 AM	*Example:* 6.5 hours
Tuesday			
Wednesday			
Thursday			
Friday			
Saturday			
Sunday			

E Exercise

Engage in at least 30 minutes of active daily movement. If you haven't worked out in a while, start with something shorter (e.g., 10 minutes) and less intense (e.g., walking). Note that you don't have to join a gym or subscribe to a class. You can do yoga, follow a YouTube Zumba class, power walk in a nearby forest, etc.

7-Day Exercise Log		
	Exercise Activity	**Time Spent**
Monday	*Example: indoor cycling*	*Example: 1 hour*
Tuesday		
Wednesday		
Thursday		
Friday		
Saturday		
Sunday		

Are you exercising enough? Y / N

If not, list down ways to increase your active hours.

Example: wake up an hour earlier, set out my exercise clothes and shoes, and put them in the bedroom, so it is the first thing I see when I wake up

I wanted to increase my daily steps, so I bought a pedometer to motivate me. If you're interested in joining a gym, then subscribe to one that's near your workplace or home.

The goal is to make exercising an "easy choice" and a seamless part of your daily routine.

1.	
2.	
3.	
4.	
5.	

Worksheet: COPE AHEAD

Coping ahead is identifying situations that are likely to make you angry. In Why Are You Angry (page 65) you listed down your anger triggers. Revisit your list, select one, and then PLAN AHEAD how to handle it. You can also write down below a specific event or situation that happened to you recently or a long time ago.

Triggering Event or Situation:

Example: Mom telling me that I am too fat.

Your turn:

_____

_____

_____

What DBT skills do you want to use to handle this situation?

Example: Wise Mind (page 25), Opposite to Emotion (page 37), DEARMAN (page 45)

Your turn:

_____

_____

_____

Imagine the situation happening RIGHT NOW.
(Be as detailed as you can.)

Example: Mom's entering the door wearing her favorite red blouse. She greets me while looking at me up and down at the same time and says, "Oh, you look like you have gained a few."

Your turn:

_____

_____

_____

Role-play; imagine in your mind how the situation is going to unfold.

Example: I excuse myself, walk to my room and quickly do Wise Mind. I decide what Opposite Action I am going to do. (I'll be cheerful because what I really want to be is defensive.) And then I am going to apply DEARMAN.

Your turn:

_____

_____

_____

Take a break. Imaginary role-playing can be mentally exhausting, and since you're thinking about a situation that angers you, it is highly possible that the role-playing itself will make you angry. As such, it is important to take a break after doing this exercise.

Example: I'll do Mindful Breathing (page 24) and then do one of my short-term BPEs (page 117).

Your turn:

_____

_____

_____

Interpersonal Effectiveness Skills for Anger Management

One of the most devastating costs of anger is the deterioration of relationships. Our volatile emotions and actions can result in lasting scars on the people we value and love the most.

In my case, I was caught in a vicious no-win situation. I felt extremely alone and isolated, which was one of the things that made me very angry. But my anger kept me from having real, deep relationships with other people. So, as the years went by, I just got lonelier and angrier.

Interacting with others has also always been so awkward for me, so I was very glad to learn the Interpersonal Effectiveness exercise Finding Friends (page 41). It was exactly what I needed to get the ball rolling in terms of meeting people and trying to forge friendships.

The fact that my personal boundaries were always being crossed at home was another big reason for my chronic anger.

In Chinese culture, there are no "boundaries." Privacy is an alien concept, and I grew up with my mom constantly barging into my room. In my parents' minds, it is *their* house, so they don't need permission to enter any of its rooms. I have also experienced my mom throwing away some of my stuff because *she* did not think they were important to me and to be respected.

In Chinese culture, we don't really "talk" about feelings. In fact, if you "talk back" to your parents, you're considered a defiant, ungrateful child, so there wasn't really much I could do in terms of setting boundaries at home. Of course, that did not mean I did not get angry when my boundaries were crossed, and since I couldn't show anger, I internalized it.

When I left home, I did not internalize my anger anymore. Whenever my boundaries were crossed, I did the exact opposite; I lashed out.

Again, I was caught in a loop. I did not communicate my boundaries, so people kept crossing them. Each time my boundaries were crossed, I would get furious.

When I finally realized the importance of setting boundaries, I got stumped again! This time, I was surprised to realize that I had trouble defining my boundaries and claiming my right to them.

So, let's start with identifying personal boundaries. After that, I'll share the DBT tools you need to start communicating them effectively so that you can get the outcomes you want from your interactions with other people.

How to Set Boundaries

"Anger is our reaction to the violation of our boundaries."—
Kathleen Dowling Singh

When our boundaries are always being crossed, we get frustrated, overwhelmed, and angry. So it is important to set healthy boundaries because they communicate what you will and will not tolerate. Note, though, that a "healthy boundary" doesn't mean saying "No" all the time. It means knowing when to say "Yes" and when to say "No."

If you're finding it difficult to figure out where you want to draw the line between yourself and other people, the following exercise is for you.

Worksheet: Anger Boundary Journaling

STEP 1. Pick an area in your life where you're often angry.

FAMILY	WORK	PARTNER
FRIENDS	DIGITAL WORLD	MYSELF

OTHER

STEP 2. Is a specific person or event making you feel this way?

Example: My older sister

Your turn: _____

STEP 3. What do you think is the underlying reason for your anger in this situation? What are you really feeling behind your anger?

(Remember, anger is a secondary emotion.)

Example: Embarrassment

Your turn: _____

STEP 4: Which boundary is being violated? (You can choose more than one.)

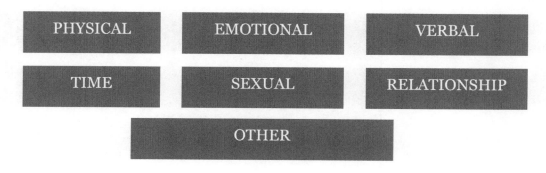

PHYSICAL	EMOTIONAL	VERBAL
TIME	SEXUAL	RELATIONSHIP

OTHER

STEP 5: Describe, in the simplest of words, your current situation. Example:

> **Area:** Family || **Person:** Sister || **Underling emotion:** Embarrassment || **Crossed Boundary:** Emotional, Relationship || **Situation:** My older sister always comments on my weight regardless of where we are, at home, while out dining, in front of friends.

Your turn:

_____

_____

_____

_____

STEP 6: Plan how you can re-instate your boundary.

Example: This is a sample plan using DEARMAN (page 45).

Describe.

For so many years, I have been receiving comments on my weight.

Express.

I feel very embarrassed each time that happens. When I was younger, I just cried about it in secret. But it is been a constant source of anger and frustration for me.

Assert.

I want that to stop.

Reinforce.

This is important to me, so I would really appreciate it if you stop commenting on my weight, especially in front of everyone.

Mindfulness.

So, I hope you understand my request.

Appear confident.

The plan: I won't apologize to my sister. I'll maintain eye contact. I'll ask her to sit, but if she stands up, I will too.

Negotiate.

If my sister is not taking me seriously, I'll say, "I understand my role in this too, you know. I have let it go on for years. So I'll understand if this doesn't change overnight. But we are adults now, so you should know how I really feel about this."

Your turn:

_____

_____

_____

_____

_____

_____

_____

_____

_____

_____

_____

_____

_____

_____

_____

_____

_____

_____

_____

_____

_____

_____

Worksheet: FAST

The following is an *assertiveness exercise*. It will teach you how to achieve your objectives, maintain relationships, and enhance self-respect. In relationships, you might sometimes go against your values and beliefs in order to be liked or get what you want. The FAST exercise will help you become more effective at self-respect.

F air.

Be reasonable when you talk about what you want and what you need. Don't get too emotional, dramatic, or talk in anger. Just stick to the facts.

Example: I don't think talking about your child's schoolmate passing away is an appropriate topic on my kid's birthday. Let's please change the subject.

NOT: Oh My God! Are you trying to sabotage my kid's birthday party?!

Your turn:

_____

_____

_____

_____

A pologies are not necessary.

Don't apologize for asking. Keep in mind that you have a right to make the request. The other person will also take you more seriously if you make your request with greater assertiveness.

Example: A kid's birthday party should be a fun, happy time, no?

NOT: I am so sorry! I did not mean to be insensitive.

Your turn:

_____

_____

_____

Stick to your values.

Don't give in merely because the other person is uncomfortable or unwilling to comply with your request. This is especially true if complying with your request would violate your moral principles or boundaries.

Example: If the guest talks about the same thing again, say, "[Name], we talked about this already. Please show some respect for my child's birthday party."

Your turn:

_____

_____

_____

_____

Truthfulness.

Don't lie or exaggerate to get what you want.

Example: I'll be more than happy to spend some time with you later to discuss. But for now, please stop.

Your turn:

_____

_____

_____

_____

Anger and Unfairness

A sense of unfairness or injustice is one of the things that make most people angry. This is because humans have an innate sense of fairness. The basic principle is really "give and receive," and in our minds, this means 50% give and 50% receive. When it is not equal, that's unfair, and we get hopping mad.

Science says that unfairness, injustice, or impartiality evolved in humans to foster cooperation.[47] When we experience unfairness, the *anterior insula* in our brain activates. This area is associated with empathy and disgust, indicating that we are hard-wired to find unfairness repulsive. In response to this injustice, the amygdala (the brain's emotional hub) is also stimulated, leading to feelings of anger and rage.

How to Deal with Unfairness

1. **Stop ruminating.** Dwelling on unfairness prolongs your own suffering from it. It does not change the situation, and by focusing on the unfairness, you're magnifying it, leading to even more feelings of rage. (**Tip**: Practical Radical Acceptance, page 103.)

2. **Cool off—literally.** Subjecting yourself physically to cold temperatures shocks your internal panic button. For example, you can splash cold water on your face, take a cold shower, hold ice cubes, and so on. (See TIPP, page 31.)

3. **Pause and think.** Anger may be our biological reaction to unfairness, but it doesn't mean we need to act on our anger impulses. Prevent the amygdala hijack from happening by using Mindfulness techniques (page 22). Often, when we take the time to think, we realize that the unfairness we perceive may not be as big or serious after all. (It may not even be there at all once you objectively and non-judgementally gather facts about the situation. (**Tip**: See Check the Facts., page 34.)

4. **Accept what's under your control and what's not.** We respond to unfairness with anger, but which aspects should we really focus on?

For example, we cannot change someone else's actions or behavior; we only have control over our own reactions. We cannot go back and relive our childhoods and correct any unfairness that happened; we can only change how we conduct ourselves as adults (today and onwards). We cannot change unfairness or tragedies that occurred in the past; we can only actively support causes that aim to prevent these in the future.

So, whenever you experience unfairness, don't dwell on "what happened?" and "this is wrong!" move to acceptance of the event (because it already happened) and then go to "how can I help?" or "how can I prevent this in the future?"

How to Prevent Yourself from Exploding

All the tools, tips, and exercises in this book to manage your anger take time and practice, so be kind and patient with yourself as you learn new behaviors. However, I do understand that in the real world, anger can come on fast and furious. Here's what my friend Melinda had to say:

"I have been ignored and taken for granted for years in my family, especially by my youngest brother. Things changed positively for me when I started working and living away from home. I started working on my deep resentment and anger issues and am happy to say that I now live a happy life with my husband and three kids. However, some days, the anger still strikes like a lightning bolt.

About a month ago, I received an SMS out of the blue from my brother, whom I hadn't spoken to in three years. No "hi" or "hello." Just "Melinda, your secretary emailed me about a paper I need to sign. I live far from the city and don't have time for this. Just figure it out." My brother lived half an hour from the city. I very calmly messaged him back that I would send my staff to him, so he's not inconvenienced in the least. He did not reply.

All of a sudden, all of my frustrations came out again: all the years of suppressing my anger to keep peace in the family, all the "giving" and "understanding" extended, all the hesitations for wanting to ask for even the smallest of things, all the changes in MY plans to accommodate theirs, all the stuff I just swallowed... I could feel my anger rising as I stared at my brother's name on my phone. I wanted to explode. But I did not.

I went into the bathroom and splashed my face with icy cold water. It was winter, so the water was really cold! I put on my winter boots and jacket and took a walk. When I came back home, I made myself a comforting cup of latte macchiato. I picked up my phone again and deleted my brother's name from the Contacts list."

When you're faced with extreme anger that catches you off-guard, don't explode. This is not because you don't have a right to your anger. This is because if you explode, you're giving up more of your power to the other person or the situation. So, here's a rapid-fire list of things to do. You don't need to do them all or in sequence. The objective is to do something quick to experience immediate relief.

1. Engage in deep, mindful breathing.

2. Cool your body down.

3. Walk away.

4. <u>Ground yourself using your five senses</u> (page 29).

5. Find a place where you can SCREAM as loud as you can.

6. Sit down and grab the armrests (or the bottom of the chair) really hard.

7. Grab a stress ball.

8. Close your eyes and go to a "happy place" (mentally escape).

9. Close and open your hands repeatedly.

10. Recite a mantra. (Examples: relax; I am in a good place now; release, release, release, and so on.)

Healthy Ways to Communicate Your Anger

You are angry. You have taken a pause, evaluated the situation and the best recourse is to communicate your anger. This doesn't mean getting physically and verbally abusive or grabbing something and throwing it at someone. These are all destructive ways of expressing anger. The following are healthy ways:

1. **"P" before "S."** Process before speaking. For example, if you're mad because your partner left the dirty dishes (yes, again!) on the kitchen counter when the dishwasher is just right there, don't shout, *"Why are you so lazy?!"* Process what the situation really makes you feel. In this example, you may feel tired (by the repeated "offense") and rejection (because you already talked to your partner about it before). Address the underlying issue.

2. **Rehearse** the conversation in your mind. (**Tip**: You can use the DEARMAN (page 45) and FAST (page 132) templates.) Using the above example, you can say, *"Babe, I saw the dishes out on the kitchen counter. I just want to explain why it frustrates me. You see, if you don't do it, it comes across to me as if you want ME to do it. You're handing the responsibility of it to me. What can we do to change this?*

3. **Do not communicate angrily.** Using angry words and having an angry demeanor will not get you the results you need. (**Tip**: See GIVE, page 48.)

4. **Do not bring up past transgressions.** We cannot change the past. Bringing up past "offenses" may only bring aggression to the discussion. Focus on moving forward.

5. **Do not mind-read.** When expressing your anger, don't jump the gun and state why you think the situation happened. (*Example: You interrupted my presentation deliberately to suck up to the boss!*) Give the other party a chance to express their views about the situation.

Anger can be very tiring and draining. It is truly worth your while to learn how to handle it effectively so that it doesn't run your life. Here's a quick rundown of what we discussed in this chapter:

- Allowing yourself to feel vulnerable is the first step to addressing your anger.
- Mindfulness is the Pause button you need to slow down the anger cycle.
- Distress Tolerance helps tolerate the situation as it is happening so that you don't explode and lash out.
- Emotion Regulation is the process of adjusting your emotions away from anger so that you're not easily controlled by it.
- Interpersonal Effectiveness is about healthy relationships with yourself and others.
- Identifying and setting your boundaries is one of the most effective ways you can prevent situations that cause anger.
- Anger can come on fast, and you may find yourself quickly on the verge of exploding. Stop yourself from it by adopting the techniques mentioned in this chapter.
- You can achieve the best results from anger when you express it in healthy ways.

In the next chapter, I'll share tips on how you can live a life less angry. Why? Learning how to handle unhealthy anger is great. But learning how to prevent it is even better!

Living a Life Less Angry

One of Dr. Marsha Linehan's goals with DBT is for people to reach a stage where they feel that life is worth living. Anger leads to so much pain and results in so much loss that it is crucial to live a life less angry!

This book has tackled so many ways to handle and get over unhealthy anger that I hope that you'll soon find more space in your life for happiness. To help you, the following are what I call my "anti-anger tips." These are life changes that I encourage you to adopt to help you get rid of unhealthy anger in your life.

HANGRY is Real

$$Hunger + Angry = Hangry$$

You know that saying? Don't argue with someone who's hungry? Well, it turns out it is true. Hunger really does make us prone to anger. A recent study showed that "hunger was associated with 37% of changes in irritability, 34% in anger and 38% in pleasure, which suggested the emotions were caused by fluctuations in hunger."[48]

The quick solution here is not to be in a situation where you experience hunger. However, we are what we eat, so what we eat also affects our moods and emotions. So, the best way is to consume a healthy, balanced meal. Here are a few tips on how you can fuel up wisely so that you don't end up fuming.

1. **Drink PLENTY of water.** Eight (8) glasses of water are the general rule, but please do adjust this depending on your height, weight, overall health, and lifestyle.

2. **Eat high-fiber foods.** These food items keep you satisfied for longer periods of time because they take time to break down in the body. High fiber foods include dark, leafy vegetables, wholegrain foods, nuts, seeds, etc.

3. **Pack healthy snacks.** When hungry, our tendency is to grab something fast and easy, which, unfortunately, almost always means something unhealthy. To resist the temptation, make it a habit to always bring healthy snacks with you, such as fruit slices, unsalted nuts, dark chocolate, etc. Meal prepping is the key here. For example, on weekends, plan your meals and snacks for the week and prepare them already.

4. **Execute "Plan B."** Forgot to pack a healthy snack? Avoid giving in to unhealthy food choices by knowing in advance where you can get healthy foods. For example, is there a *Subway* sandwich store nearby? If so, know the healthiest option there. "Plan B" is thus, head onto Subway and order *x*.

5. **Don't skip meals.** Skipping meals leads to hangry. In addition, it slows down your metabolism and may even cause you to overeat on your next meal.

Note: The above list is not comprehensive. Nutrition is a very broad and deep topic beyond this book's scope. Please talk to your doctor or a nutritionist to receive proper and customized nutritional advice.

Get Enough Sleep!

The importance of a good night's sleep is possibly today's most underrated health habit, and science reveals that sleep debt can increase feelings of anger.[49] Unfortunately, we do not sleep enough. Adults, according to the Centers for Disease Control and Prevention (CDC), should sleep for at least seven hours every night. However, over 60% of adults around the world say they don't sleep as well as they want.[50]

Following are a few tips on how to get enough good quality sleep.

1. **Turn off your screens** at least an hour before bed. The hormone that makes us feel tired, *melatonin*, is not produced as a result of the blue light from our displays. Using an app like *Twilight* for your phone or *f.lux* for your laptop is a good place to start.

2. **Unwind before going to bed** by reading a book, listening to soothing music, or engaging in meditation or light yoga.

3. **Make your bedroom conducive to sleeping.** Today's bedrooms are multi-purpose (e.g., workplace, children's playroom, etc.) Bring it back to its original purpose by de-cluttering, installing dim lights, hanging blackout curtains, and removing all devices.

4. **Cool down your bedroom.** Room temperatures between 60 and 67°F is best for Rapid Eye Movement (REM) sleep, the stage where dreaming, learning, memory, emotional processing, and healthy brain development occurs. If your room is too hot or too cold, you'll keep waking up, which prevents you from reaching REM and deep, restorative sleep.

5. **Practice gratitude.** You can write your positive thoughts on a journal you keep beside your bed, or you can simply lie down, close your eyes, and just mentally list down the people, events, and things for which you are grateful that day. Personally, doing this relaxes my body and mind, and I fall asleep mid-way.

Be Accountable for Your Own Emotions

"Why does he make me so angry all the time?!"

"Why does mom always invade my privacy?!"

"Argh! Why did my boss give such impossible deadlines?!"

"This is crazy! Why is that checkout lady so slow? Can't she see this line is so damn long?"

When we are angry, the tendency is to assign blame. Someone or something caused feelings of rage... as if we don't have a say in our own emotions. In truth, external factors *prompt* our anger, but when we are in an actual angry state, that's on us.

Anger is a *personal* emotional state. It is based on your personal preferences, prejudices, and life experiences. This is why what infuriates you might not bother anyone else at all.

So the next time you feel anger, try not to look outward. Take responsibility for your own emotions and try to figure out WHY you have allowed yourself to be angered by the situation. Whatever happened, you are entirely accountable for what happens next.

Assigning blame:
 "Why does Adrian make me so angry all the time?!"
Taking responsibility for your emotions:
"I am easily angered by Adrian because he reminds me of an abusive ex."

Assigning blame:
"Why does mom always invade my privacy?!"
Taking responsibility for your emotions:
"I need to have a serious talk with mom about my boundaries."

Assigning blame:
"Argh! Why did my boss give such impossible deadlines?!"
Taking responsibility for your emotions:
"I knew the deadlines when the project started. I am super frustrated because I did not speak up during meetings about why the deadlines were impossible to meet."

Assigning blame:

"This is crazy! Why is that checkout lady so slow? Can't she see this line is so damn long?"

Taking responsibility for your emotions:

"I could have gone shopping during non-peak hours, but I chose this moment even though I KNOW it is always busy here at this time. So, I guess I am really just angry at myself. LOL."

Setbacks

Things don't always go as planned. Setbacks happen. And when they do, it is easy to get flustered and angry.

When setbacks happen, one way to combat any negative reactions is to practice *gratitude*. For example, instead of getting mad at yourself because you gained two pounds, be happy and grateful that you lost 10 pounds the month before. Instead of focusing on the fact that your friends are "always late" for lunch dates, focus on the fact that they are your true friends who would do anything for you.

Another technique is called *reframing*, which is changing the way you look at things. For example, instead of being furious that you missed a turn and added 20 minutes to your drive, reframe the situation by thinking, *"I have actually always been intrigued by this route. I guess today I'll finally get to see it."* Here's another example: your neighbor shrieks at the presence of your cat outside, and you hear a nasty swear word against you come out. Instead of getting mad, think, *"That's got nothing to do with me or Elsa (the cat). He's just having a bad day."*

Let It Go

Imagine a cup on your desk. If you fill it up with anger, it will overflow, spill out all over your desk and ruin all the papers you have spread in front of you. You need to "throw out" or release your anger so that you can your cup is ready to receive new, healthy, and positive emotions. Here are some tips on how you can let go of anger.

1. **Start from a place of peace.** Breathe, relax, and calm yourself. (See Distress Tolerance, page 28.)

2. **Check your perspective.** When we are angry, everything is magnified. Check the facts (page 34) and see if they fit the level of your anger.

3. **Go ahead and comfort yourself.** Cuddle with your pet, buy a plant, re-watch your favorite Netflix series, etc.

4. **Write down what you feel.** Don't censor yourself and let it all out. Put into writing the words and emotions that want to explode from you, and then burn the piece of paper.

5. **Get a birthday balloon**, blow it out and then pop it.

6. **Light a candle.** Stare at the flame. Make it the target of your rage, and then blow the candle out.

7. Express your anger in healthy ways (page 137).

8. **Forgive**. Many people think forgiveness is giving others a pass. However, I have come to realize that forgiveness is actually very healing for the *forgiver*.

Most, if not all, of my anger issues stem from my childhood. But I cannot go back and change that. Holding a grudge against my parents is also not the solution because it just makes me a prisoner of my childhood and prolongs my suffering. So, I have chosen to forgive. I did not have a sit down with my family and said, "*I forgive you guys*." Instead, one day, I found myself sitting on a park bench, and I just acknowledged that my immigrant parents were doing the best they could with what they had and knew, and I said, "*I forgive*".

Live a Positive Life

"Darkness cannot drive out darkness: only light can do that." –
Martin Luther King Jr.

When you fill your life with light, darkness has a very hard time penetrating it. Truth be told, when I started this journey, my only goal was to stop being angry. Anger was just costing me too much. As I started to change, I found many aspects of life improving too. So my final tip to live a life less angry is to live a life more happy.

1. **Ask yourself what makes you happy**. So many people want to be happy and yet have a very hard time identifying exactly what makes them happy. I should know; I was one of them. So ask yourself what makes you happy, and don't just focus on the "big stuff." In fact, go for the simple stuff first, and then do your best to fill your days with a lot of these "little things."

Here are a few of the things that make me happy and how I have expanded them to amplify my happiness.

- A strong, hot cup of coffee in the morning.

  So I invested in a good coffee machine. I also figured out what coffee beans I liked best and started buying only that.

- A nice, tasty smear of butter on really good bread.

  I switched to grass-fed butter and started buying artisan bread from a local bakery.

- People greeting me on my long forest walks.

  I don't wait to be greeted anymore. I initiate it.

2. Set and claim your **boundaries**. (**Tip**: See <u>How to Set Boundaries</u> on page 128.)

3. Engage in **self-care**. Exercise daily and eat well for your health. Ask for help when you need it. Take breaks more often. Read a book just because. Get enough sleep. Say no if you want to. Say yes if you want to. Don't bother with what other people think of you. Smile.

4. **LIKE yourself.** This may come as a surprise, but many people don't like themselves or what they've become. Somehow, it became common and okay to self-bash and self-criticize. One way to counter this is to talk to yourself as you would a friend: be gentle, be kind, and be supportive.

Why don't you do this right now? Write down three (3) things you like and appreciate about yourself.

Examples:
I like how I make people smile.
I like how I love taking long walks and appreciate nature.
I like how I'm open to learning new behaviors to control my anger.

1. _____

2. _____

3. _____

 # 5. Leave the past. Don't live in the past because that means you miss today, and you'll cloud tomorrow. "Leave the past" is not just about letting go. It's also about consciously, deliberately living in the moment. Most people are either thinking about the past or worrying about the future, and that just makes you miss today, doesn't it? So, just enjoy and live today to its fullest.

6. Acknowledge your **accomplishments**.

Why don't you do this right now? Write down three (3) accomplishments you did the past week that you're proud of. It doesn't matter what they are or if they're "big" or "small" accomplishments.

Examples:
I took 10,000 steps a day for five (5) consecutive days.
I took a chance and volunteered to lead our latest marketing campaign at work.
I started waking up 15 minutes earlier than usual.

1. _____
2. _____
3. _____

7. Wake up expecting **happiness** and go to sleep practicing **gratitude**.

8. Build and keep **healthy relationships**, and end toxic ones. For example, call up an old friend you haven't communicated with in a while, message three (3) friends, ask them how they are and let them know you're thinking about them, block a bully on social media, delete and block an ex who has been harassing you, and so on.

Please go ahead and add your own ideas to living a positive life.

_____

_____

_____

_____

_____

Conclusion

An angry life is a hard one to live. I am filled with gratitude that you have chosen this book to guide you to live a life less angry. Again, please remember that addressing anger is not a linear process. There will be roadblocks and setbacks, but nothing that you cannot overcome.

Here's a quick recap of all that we covered in this book:

- Dialectic Behavior Therapy (DBT) and its main fundamentals (Acceptance and Change) and its core skills (Mindfulness, Distress Tolerance, Emotion Regulation, and Interpersonal Effectiveness).
- What anger is: what happens in the brain when anger is triggered, the anger cycle, and the basic differences in anger in men and women.
- Understanding the source of your anger (Why Are You Angry?) and how you may be destructively expressing it.
- The physical, emotional, mental, social, financial, and relationship costs of anger.
- The DBT tools and skills you can apply to effectively manage anger in your life.
- How you can live a life focused on happiness and not anger.

Learning new behaviors is never easy, but it is not impossible. You got this book because you know that anger is not good for you. So please keep on trying to manage your anger because that is what's good for you.

What we think, we become. – Buddha

Appendix A – Miller-Patton Anger Self-Assessment

The **Miller-Patton Anger Self-Assessment** exercise was created by licensed marriage and family therapists Mark S. Miller, MA, and Patricia Patton, Ph.D. of Emerge from Anger.[51]

Warning: This self-assessment explores aspects of anger and contains depictions of self-harm, alcohol abuse, eating disorders, and others. Please read with care.

If you agree with the statement, circle TRUE; if you disagree, circle FALSE. If any statement is not applicable to you (i.e., statements related to partners), you can skip them.

STATEMENT	True or False?	
1. I use foul language, including slurs, sarcasm, and name-calling.	True	False
2. People say I become furious too easily.	True	False
3. It takes me a very long time to cool down.	True	False
4. I still get upset when I reflect on the wrongdoings of people against me or the unfairness of life.	True	False
5. I frequently criticize and judge other people, even when they don't seek my opinion or assistance.	True	False
6. To stop people from nagging me, I engage in passive-aggressive tactics like ignoring them or making promises to do things, only to "forget" about them.	True	False
7. I make aggressive gestures and attitudes, such as clenching my fists, glaring at others, making banging noises, and others.	True	False
8. I spend a lot of time thinking about what scathing responses I should have made at the time or how I can exact revenge when someone does or says something that enrages me.	True	False
9. Following an angry outburst, I resort to self-destructive activities to calm down, such as gambling, excessive eating, vomiting, or self-harm.	True	False
10. Sometimes, after an occurrence that makes me really upset, I get physical sickness (headaches, nausea, vomiting, diarrhea, etc.).	True	False

STATEMENT	True or False?	
11. Forgiving someone who has wronged me is really difficult, nearly impossible. Even if they have expressed regret and made an effort to make amends, I just can't give them a pass and forgive.	True	False
12. I constantly have to win a debate and establish my "rightness."	True	False
13. I frequently rationalize my actions and attribute my irrational conduct to other individuals or external factors (like job stress, financial problems, etc.)	True	False
14. When I am frustrated, I respond so negatively that I ruminate, or I have trouble falling asleep at night because I keep thinking about the things that have upset me.	True	False
15. I frequently despise myself for losing my anger after arguing with someone.	True	False
16. There are moments when I am so enraged that I "see red" and think of killing someone or myself.	True	False
17. I occasionally lose track of what I say or do when I am angry.	True	False
18. I am aware that some people "walk on eggshells" around me to avoid upsetting me because they are terrified of me when I get angry.	True	False
19. When I have been furious, I have slammed doors, hurled things, smashed things, or	True	False

STATEMENT	True or False?	
punched walls.		
20. Even when there was no proof that my partner was being unfaithful, I was unnecessarily possessive and jealous of them, accusing them of cheating.	True	False
21. On occasion, I have had my partner perform sexual acts they don't want to, or I have threatened to cheat on them if they don't comply with my demands in order to satisfy my sexual needs.	True	False
22. I have occasionally chosen to ignore my spouse in an effort to hurt them while being extra kind to other family members or friends.	True	False
23. In order to exert control and manipulate my partner's emotions and behavior, I have made them dependent on me or socially isolated. This has prevented them from leaving me or ending our relationship.	True	False
24. I have threatened people in order to get my way or win a debate.	True	False
25. I feel like I have been betrayed a lot in the past, and I find it very hard to trust people.	True	False

Scoring the Miller-Patton Anger Self-Assessment Quiz

Important: The Miller-Patton Anger Self-Assessment test is an informal screening test to help you learn more about your emotions and outward displays of anger. It is NOT meant to be a formal evaluation.

- If you circled **True** to 10 or more of the statements above, you most likely suffer from moderate-to-severe anger issues.
- If you circled **True** to five of the statements above, you are most likely at risk of having an anger problem.
- Even if you circled **True** to only one of the questions, it would still be beneficial for you to learn the anger management techniques in this book to improve your coping skills.
- If you circled **True** to **Statement #16** and believe you may engage in self-harm, please dial 911 (or your local support hotline) for immediate assistance.

Review Request

If you enjoyed this book or found it useful...

I'd like to ask you for a quick favor:

Please share your thoughts and leave a quick REVIEW. Your feedback matters and helps me make improvements to provide the best books possible.

Reviews are so helpful to both readers and authors, so any help would be greatly appreciated! You can leave a review here:

https://tinyurl.com/dbt-anger-review

Or by scanning the QR code below:

Also, please join my ARC team to get early access to my releases.

https://barretthuang.com/arc-team/

THANK YOU!

Further Reading
DBT Workbook for Adults

Develop Emotional Wellbeing with Practical Exercises for Managing Fear, Stress, Worry, Anxiety, Panic Attacks, Intrusive Thoughts & More

(Includes 12-Week Plan for Anxiety Relief)

Get it here:

https://tinyurl.com/dbtadult

Or by scanning the QR code below:

DBT Workbook For Kids

Fun & Practical Dialectal Behavior Therapy Skills Training For Children

Help Kids Recognize Their Emotions, Manage Anxiety & Phobias, and Learn To Thrive!

Get it here:

https://tinyurl.com/dbtkids

Or by scanning the QR code below:

DBT Workbook For Teens

A Complete Dialectical Behavior Therapy Toolkit

Essential Coping Skills and Practical Activities To Help Teenagers & Adolescents Manage Stress, Anxiety, ADHD, Phobias & More

Get it here:

https://tinyurl.com/dbt-teens

Or by scanning the QR code below:

About the Author

Barrett Huang is an author and businessman. Barrett spent years discovering the best ways to manage his OCD, overcoming his anxiety, and learning to embrace life. Through his writing, he hopes to share his knowledge with readers, empowering people of all backgrounds with the tools and strategies they need to improve their mental wellbeing and be happy and healthy.

When not writing or running his business, Barrett loves to spend his time studying. He has majored in psychology and completed the DBT skills certificate course by Dr. Marsha Linehan. Barrett's idol is Bruce Lee, who said, "The key to immortality is first living a life worth remembering."

Learn more about Barrett's books here:
https://barretthuang.com/

Index

References

1 Linehan, M. (2015). *DBT skills training manual*. The Guilford Press.

2 Carey, B. (2011, June 23). *Expert on mental illness reveals her own fight*. The New York Times. Retrieved August 1, 2022, from https://www.nytimes.com/2011/06/23/health/23lives.html

3 Influence Digest. (2018, February 9). *Research has shown that you can condition yourself to do anything*. Influence Digest. Retrieved August 1, 2022, from https://influencedigest.com/psychology/research-shown-condition-yourself-anything/

4 Linehan, M. M., & Dimeff, L. (2001). Dialectical Behavior Therapy in a Nutshell. The California Psychologist. https://www.ebrightcollaborative.com/uploads/2/3/3/9/23399186/dbtinanutshell.pdf

5 Levine, M. (2012, July 12). *Logic and emotion: Delving into the logical and emotional sides of the human brain*. Psychology Today. Retrieved August 1, 2022, from https://www.psychologytoday.com/intl/blog/the-divided-mind/201207/logic-and-emotion

6 Holt-Lunstad, J., Smith, T. B., & Layton, J. B. (2010). Social relationships and mortality risk: A meta-analytic review. *PLoS Medicine, 7*(7). https://doi.org/10.1371/journal.pmed.1000316

7 Mejia, Z. (2018, March 20). *Harvard's longest study of adult life reveals how you can be happier and more successful*. CNBC. Retrieved August 1, 2022, from https://www.cnbc.com/2018/03/20/this-harvard-study-reveals-how-you-can-be-happier-and-more-successful.html

8 Byrne, D. (1961). Interpersonal attraction and attitude similarity. *The Journal of Abnormal and Social Psychology, 62*(3), 713–715. https://doi.org/10.1037/h0044721

9 Montoya, R. M., Horton, R. S., & Kirchner, J. (2008). Is actual similarity necessary for attraction? A meta-analysis of actual and perceived similarity. *Journal of Social and Personal Relationships, 25*(6), 889–922. https://doi.org/10.1177/0265407508096700

10 Laursen, B. (2017). Making and keeping friends: The importance of being similar. *Child Development Perspectives, 11*(4), 282–289. https://doi.org/10.1111/cdep.12246

11 Frazier, S. N., & Vela, J. (2014). Dialectical behavior therapy for the treatment of anger and aggressive behavior: A Review. *Aggression and Violent Behavior, 19*(2), 156–163. https://doi.org/10.1016/j.avb.2014.02.001

12 Wright, S., Day, A., & Howells, K. (2009). Mindfulness and the treatment of Anger Problems. *Aggression and Violent Behavior, 14*(5), 396–401. https://doi.org/10.1016/j.avb.2009.06.008

13 Momeni, J., Omidi, A., Raygan, F., & Akbari, H. (2016). The effects of mindfulness-based stress reduction on cardiac patients' blood pressure, perceived stress, and anger: A single-blind randomized controlled trial. *Journal of the American Society of Hypertension, 10*(10), 763–771. https://doi.org/10.1016/j.jash.2016.07.007

14 DeSteno, D., Lim, D., Duong, F., & Condon, P. (2017). Meditation inhibits aggressive responses to provocations. *Mindfulness, 9*(4), 1117–1122. https://doi.org/10.1007/s12671-017-0847-2

15 Onyedibe, M. C., Ibeagha, P. N., & Onyishi, I. E. (2019). Distress tolerance moderates the relationship between anger experience and elevated blood pressure. *South African Journal of Psychology, 50*(1), 39–53. https://doi.org/10.1177/0081246319832540

16 Hawkins, K. A., Macatee, R. J., Guthrie, W., & Cougle, J. R. (2012). Concurrent and prospective relations between distress tolerance, life stressors, and anger. *Cognitive Therapy and Research, 37*(3), 434–445. https://doi.org/10.1007/s10608-012-9487-y

17 Ellis, A. J., Vanderlind, W. M., & Beevers, C. G. (2012). Enhanced anger reactivity and reduced distress tolerance in major depressive disorder. *Cognitive Therapy and Research, 37*(3), 498–509. https://doi.org/10.1007/s10608-012-9494-z

18 Mauss, I. B., Cook, C. L., & Gross, J. J. (2007). Automatic emotion regulation during anger provocation. *Journal of Experimental Social Psychology, 43*(5), 698–711. https://doi.org/10.1016/j.jesp.2006.07.003

19 Renna, M. E., Quintero, J. M., Fresco, D. M., & Mennin, D. S. (2017). Emotion regulation therapy: A mechanism-targeted treatment for disorders of distress. *Frontiers in Psychology, 8*. https://doi.org/10.3389/fpsyg.2017.00098

20 Fabiansson, E. C., & Denson, T. F. (2012). The effects of intrapersonal anger and its regulation in economic bargaining. *PLoS ONE, 7*(12). https://doi.org/10.1371/journal.pone.0051595

21 Goleman, D. (2006). *Emotional intelligence: Why it can matter more than Iq.* Bantam Books.

22 ScienceDaily. (2000, January 31). *Comparison of anger expression in men and women reveals surprising differences.* ScienceDaily. Retrieved September 3, 2022, from https://www.sciencedaily.com/releases/2000/01/000131075609.htm

23 Esquire (Ed.). (2020, August 21). *American rage: The 'esquire'/nbc news survey.* Esquire. Retrieved September 1, 2022, from https://www.esquire.com/news-politics/a40693/american-rage-nbc-survey/

24 Brescoll, V. L., & Uhlmann, E. L. (2008). Can an angry woman get ahead? *Psychological Science, 19*(3), 268–275. https://doi.org/10.1111/j.1467-9280.2008.02079.x

25 Casper, R. F. (2021). *Patient education: Premenstrual syndrome (PMS) and premenstrual dysphoric disorder (PMDD) (Beyond the Basics).* UpToDate. Retrieved September 1, 2022, from https://www.uptodate.com/contents/premenstrual-syndrome-pms-and-premenstrual-dysphoric-disorder-pmdd-beyond-the-basics

26 Yeşildere Sağlam, H., & Basar, F. (2019). The relationship between premenstrual syndrome and anger. *Pakistan Journal of Medical Sciences, 35*(2). https://doi.org/10.12669/pjms.35.2.232

27 Lerner, J. S., Gonzalez, R. M., Small, D. A., & Fischhoff, B. (2003). Effects of fear and anger on perceived risks of terrorism. *Psychological Science, 14*(2), 144–150. https://doi.org/10.1111/1467-9280.01433

28 Reilly, P. M., & Shopshire, M. S. (2019). ANGER MANAGEMENT for Substance Use Disorder and Mental Health Clients. Rockville, MD; U.S. Department of Health and Human Services.

29 Lisitsa, E., Fraser, C., & Benson, K. (n.d.). *A research-based approach to relationships.* The Gottman Institute. Retrieved September 1, 2022, from https://www.gottman.com/

30 *Nicole Lippman-Barile, Ph.D on mindbodygreen.* mindbodygreen. (n.d.). Retrieved September 1, 2022, from https://www.mindbodygreen.com/wc/nicole-lippman-barile-ph-d

31 Kawachi, I., Sparrow, D., Spiro, A., Vokonas, P., & Weiss, S. T. (1996). A prospective study of anger and coronary heart disease. *Circulation, 94*(9), 2090–2095. https://doi.org/10.1161/01.cir.94.9.2090

32 Davidson, K. W., & Mostofsky, E. (2010). Anger expression and risk of coronary heart disease: Evidence from the Nova Scotia Health Survey. *American Heart Journal, 159*(2), 199–206. https://doi.org/10.1016/j.ahj.2009.11.007

33 Montenegro, C. E., & Montenegro, S. T. (2018). Anger and cardiovascular disease: An old and complicated relationship. *Arquivos Brasileiros De Cardiologia.* https://doi.org/10.5935/abc.20180176

34 Baumeister, R. F., & Leary, M. R. (1995). The need to belong: Desire for interpersonal attachments as a fundamental human motivation. *Psychological Bulletin, 117*(3), 497–529. https://doi.org/10.1037/0033-2909.117.3.497

35 Over, H. (2016). The origins of belonging: Social Motivation in infants and young children. *Philosophical Transactions of the Royal Society B: Biological Sciences, 371*(1686), 20150072. https://doi.org/10.1098/rstb.2015.0072

36 Williams, V. (2022, March 4). *Mayo Clinic Minute: The benefits of being socially connected - mayo clinic news network.* Mayo Clinic. Retrieved September 1, 2022, from https://newsnetwork.mayoclinic.org/discussion/mayo-clinic-minute-the-benefits-of-being-socially-connected/

37 Lin, S., Faust, L., Robles-Granda, P., Kajdanowicz, T., & Chawla, N. V. (2019). Social network structure is predictive of Health and Wellness. *PLOS ONE, 14*(6). https://doi.org/10.1371/journal.pone.0217264

38 Adler, A. B., LeardMann, C. A., Yun, S., Jacobson, I. G., & Forbes, D. (2022). Problematic anger and economic difficulties: Findings from the Millennium Cohort Study. *Journal of Affective Disorders, 297,* 679–685. https://doi.org/10.1016/j.jad.2021.10.078

39 Ngo, S. (2016, February 22). *How anger can hurt your finances.* Wall St. Watchdog. Retrieved September 8, 2022, from

https://www.wallstwatchdog.com/money-career/how-anger-can-hurt-your-finances/

40 South Richardson, D. (2014). Everyday aggression takes many forms. *Current Directions in Psychological Science, 23*(3), 220–224. https://doi.org/10.1177/0963721414530143

41 Arslan, G. (2021). School belongingness, well-being, and mental health among adolescents: Exploring the role of loneliness. *Australian Journal of Psychology, 73*(1), 70–80. https://doi.org/10.1080/00049530.2021.1904499

42 Taren, A. A., Creswell, J. D., & Gianaros, P. J. (2013). Dispositional mindfulness co-varies with smaller amygdala and caudate volumes in community adults. *PLoS ONE, 8*(5). https://doi.org/10.1371/journal.pone.0064574

43 *Anger styles are learned.* Mental Help Anger Styles Are Learned Comments. (n.d.). Retrieved September 1, 2022, from https://www.mentalhelp.net/anger/types/

44 Pally, R., & Olds, D. (2018). Emotional processing: The mind-body connection. *The Mind-Brain Relationship, 73*–104. https://doi.org/10.4324/9780429482465-4

45 Watson, N. F., Badr, M. S., Belenky, G., Bliwise, D. L., Buxton, O. M., Buysse, D., Dinges, D. F., Gangwisch, J., Grandner, M. A., Kushida, C., Malhotra, R. K., Martin, J. L., Patel, S. R., Quan, S., & Tasali, E. (2015). Recommended amount of sleep for a healthy adult: A joint consensus statement of the American Academy of Sleep Medicine and Sleep Research Society. *SLEEP.* https://doi.org/10.5665/sleep.4716

46 Saghir, Z., Syeda, J. N., Muhammad, A. S., & Balla Abdalla, T. (2018). The amygdala, sleep debt, sleep deprivation, and the emotion of anger: A possible connection? *Cureus.* https://doi.org/10.7759/cureus.2912

47 Brosnan, S. F., & de Waal, F. B. (2014). Evolution of responses to (un)fairness. *Science, 346*(6207). https://doi.org/10.1126/science.1251776

48 Swami, V., Hochstöger, S., Kargl, E., & Stieger, S. (2022). Hangry in the field: An experience sampling study on the impact of hunger on anger, irritability, and affect. *PLOS ONE, 17*(7). https://doi.org/10.1371/journal.pone.0269629

49 Krizan, Z., & Hisler, G. (2019). Sleepy anger: Restricted sleep amplifies angry feelings. *Journal of Experimental Psychology: General, 148*(7), 1239–1250. https://doi.org/10.1037/xge0000522

50 Philips Global Sleep Survey. (2019). The global pursuit of better sleep health. Source: https://www.usa.philips.com/c-dam/b2c/master/experience/smartsleep/world-sleep-day/2019/2019-philips-world-sleep-day-survey-results.pdf

51 *Marriage and family therapist: Emerge from anger: Santa Clarita.* Emergefromanger1. (n.d.). Retrieved September 1, 2022, from https://www.emergefromanger.com/

Made in the USA
Monee, IL
02 February 2025

11366478R00092